Liberating
Evangelism

Christian Mission and Modern Culture

EDITED BY
ALAN NEELY, H. WAYNE PIPKIN,
AND WILBERT R. SHENK

In the series:

Liberating Evangelism

Gospel, Theology, and the Dynamics of Communication

STEPHEN K. PICKARD

TRINITY PRESS INTERNATIONAL
Harrisburg, Pennsylvania

Trinity Press International, P.O. Box 1321, Harrisburg, PA 17105
Trinity Press International is a division of the Morehouse Group.

Library of Congress Cataloging-in-Publication Data

Pickard, Stephen K.
    Liberating evangelism : gospel, theology, and the dynamics of communication / Stephen K. Pickard.
        p.   cm. – (Christian mission and modern culture)
    Includes bibliographical references.
    ISBN 1-56338-279-2 (pbk. : alk. paper)
    1. Evangelistic work – Philosophy.   I. Title.   II. Series.
BV3793.P46 1999
269'.2 – dc21   99-26134

Printed in the United States of America

99   00   01   02   03   04   10   9   8   7   6   5   4   3   2   1

Contents

97141

Preface to the Series

Both Christian mission and modern culture, widely regarded as antagonists, are in crisis. The emergence of the modern mission movement in the early nineteenth century cannot be understood apart from the rise of technocratic society. Now, at the end of the twentieth century, both modern culture and Christian mission face an uncertain future.

One of the developments integral to modernity was the way the role of religion in culture was redefined. Whereas religion had played an authoritative role in the culture of Christendom, modern culture was highly critical of religion and increasingly secular in its assumptions. A sustained effort was made to banish religion to the backwaters of modern culture.

The decade of the 1980s witnessed further momentous developments on the geopolitical front with the collapse of communism. In the aftermath of the breakup of the system of power blocs that dominated international relations for a generation, it is clear that religion has survived even if its institutionalization has undergone deep change and its future forms are unclear. Secularism continues to oppose religion, while technology has emerged as a major source of power and authority in modern culture. Both confront Christian faith with fundamental questions.

The purpose of this series is to probe these developments

from a variety of angles with a view to helping the church understand its missional responsibility to a culture in crisis. One important resource is the church's experience of two centuries of cross-cultural mission that has reshaped the church into a global Christian *ecumene*. The focus of our inquiry will be the church in modern culture. The series (1) examines modern/postmodern culture from a missional point of view; (2) develops the theological agenda that the church in modern culture must address in order to recover its own integrity; and (3) tests fresh conceptualizations of the nature and mission of the church as it engages modern culture. In other words, these volumes are intended to be a forum where conventional assumptions can be challenged and alternative formulations explored.

This series is a project authorized by the Institute of Mennonite Studies, research agency of the Associated Mennonite Biblical Seminary, and supported by a generous grant from the Pew Charitable Trusts.

Editorial Committee

ALAN NEELY
H. WAYNE PIPKIN
WILBERT R. SHENK

Acknowledgments

I began this volume while I was lecturing at United Theological College in Sydney. I am grateful for the support and encouragement of my former faculty colleagues in the undertaking of this project. I especially wish to thank Wilbert Shenk for the invitation to write in the series. I am indebted to the following people for their willingness to read and respond to the manuscript: Sarah Mitchell, William Emilsen, Gordon and Ruth Dicker, Dean Drayton, Ian Robinson, Richard Lennan, and Wayne Pipkin. I am indebted to all those bearers of the gospel in word and deed who enrich and energize my own pilgrimage, especially Jennifer, Ruth, Miriam, and Andrew. None of the aforementioned bear responsibility for what I have written.

Introduction

Evangelist: Who Me?

Some years ago in Durham, England, a member of a small group I belonged to in my local church said he had never experienced God's presence as a gushing torrent of water. This older and wise friend likened God's activity in his life to the constant drip of water from a leaky tap. The glad tidings of the gospel had molded his life and had a great impact on his Christian witness. He was not the gushy type, but his life spoke more clearly of the gospel than did many sermons. I suspect he was not comfortable with the "evangelism" word, though I am quite sure that the pulse of the evangel flowed through his Christian discipleship. His story and the memorable image he offered would resonate with many today who feel that evangelism is not for them.

In my own case I was fortunate to be nurtured in the Christian faith from early days through the influence of my parents and local church. However, it was in my early twenties that I began to discover in quite dramatic manner how satisfying the way of Jesus could be: "a spring of water welling up to eternal life" (John 4:14b). The praise of God seemed to flow freely, effortlessly, even unself-consciously. The tag of Christian could be owned with a new confidence and joy.

What about being an evangelist? Was this something I had to be? There were a number of evangelists around at the time, but I found their methods unattractive. Was this simply a question of personality? I have since met countless people who have said evangelism was not for them; they were not the type. However, this experience raises some serious questions for me. Has the church simply abdicated its responsibility and privilege for the spread of the gospel? Has this baptismal birthright been forgotten or denied out of ignorance, poor example, or even misinformation? What I am sure of is that the church is called to be a community of the evangel and thus a community that seeks to embody the glad tidings of God in all its life. Although not all might be called as evangelists in the narrower sense of that term, all are called to be bearers of the good news in deeds and words. Such a task and joy cannot be siphoned off for those who fit the type! Evangelism denotes a calling at the heart of Christian discipleship in the world. It is a calling for men and women of every type, race, language, and color. The laborers for the harvest are far greater in quality and quantity than is often believed to be the case. They need to be freed to be bearers of glad tidings. Evangelism needs to be liberated from false and restrictive notions. As this occurs, many people will discover joy and confidence in the gospel, and many more will be surprised and delighted in their inmost being to discover that the evangel truly liberates. This points to the variety of ways in which the title of this book, *Liberating Evangelism,* can be understood. They all will be found relevant in the following chapters.

Evangelism: Another Ism in the Church?

There are signs in the church today that the recovery of the evangelism imperative is gaining momentum, particularly at the local level. Can Christian theology join in this recovery and make its own contribution? I believe it can and moreover that theologians of the church have a responsibility to play their part in this movement of the Spirit. My own pilgrimage in theology has been in the area of systematics, a field that has a responsibility to offer as clear and intelligent an account of the Christian faith as is possible. This requires an attentive listening to the contemporary situation and faithfulness to the gospel, its tradition of interpretation and praxis in the Christian community through history. Accordingly, when I refer to theology in the following chapters, my primary concern is with the enterprise of systematic theology. The specific question I bring to the field of evangelism is this: What might a contemporary theology of evangelism look like? This larger question provides the basic framework for the discussion that follows. In order to address this quite fundamental question, I have chosen to explore two issues relevant and critical for a contemporary theology of evangelism. The first concerns the relationship between evangelism and systematic theology. The second and related issue concerns the relationship of evangelism to the church.

Why these two issues? The short answer is that I believe that evangelism, church, and theology belong together; the loss of connectedness has been detrimental for all three. What the church is and what it does are intimately related to what has gone under the name of evangelism, and for very good reason. At its heart, the church is called to be the community of the evangel bearing the glad tidings of God in the world. Therefore, evangelism is not just another ism for the church to take on board. Yet, as indicated above, that is precisely how evangelism is perceived by many people of the church. The reasons for this are many, for example, poor or naive views of evangelism, and experience with some dubious evangelistic practices. For some, the sense that the church has lost its way has been a major driving force behind many well-intentioned but inappropriate and even harmful evangelistic practices. In reaction, many people effectively give up any responsibility for the good news beyond their own privileged walls, or they transpose evangelism into other activities (e.g., social action) and dissipate its energy. This has led Walter Brueggemann to state: "Part of the task concerning evangelism is to recover nerve about our modes of speech in church traditions that have debased our speech, either by conservative reductionism or by liberal embarrassment" (1993:14). Given this state of affairs, at least in the Western world, a number of integrations will be necessary if the authentic voice of the people of God is to be recovered and the evangel can be experienced as genuinely *good* news.

In this volume, as indicated above, I deal with two necessary integrations. The first involves forging a new link between evangelism and theology. For too long the theory and the practice of the gospel have been disconnected. Evangelism has been deprived of a critical stimulus, and theology has forgotten that its impulse and source is nothing less than "the truth that is in Jesus" (Eph. 4:21). The rupture between these two callings of the Christian church has been serious and harmful. What is required is a recovery of the genuinely complementary nature of these two forms of gospel communication. What this might involve and how it may benefit the church's evangelistic task is introduced in Chapter 1 and is further developed in terms of the dynamics of communication in Chapters 2 and 3.

A second integration required for the renewal of evangelism involves the church. Evangelism has to be firmly related to the concrete existence of the Christian church.

The effects of severing the connection between evangelism and the church have been twofold: an introverted church life and the relegation of evangelism to the outskirts of the Christian community. Overcoming the separation is a two-way movement. The locus for evangelism will have to be the Christian community — its life of worship and discipleship in the world. The church will have to be reconceived missiologically, for example, in terms of the Matthean "Great Commission" (Shenk 1995:108). Chapter 4 explores this double movement by focusing on the character of the church as a community for the praise of God. The theme of praise and its relevance for evangelism is developed further in Chapter 5. This final chapter explores an approach to evangelism that is "praise-centered."

A theme running through the inquiry into evangelism, theology, and church concerns the way in which the gospel is communicated. This is not simply an issue of finding the right technique to communicate the gospel in our modern world. The primary concern is to uncover how the gospel actually works — its own inner logic and dynamic. I argue that the communicative dynamic of the gospel requires a vigorous theological engagement with the gospel and a church energized and directed by the God to whom it offers praise. The Christian tradition has identified the twin coordinates for this praise: the life, death, and resurrection of Jesus of Nazareth and the ongoing presence and action of God's Holy Spirit. As evangelism takes its cue from a community of people formed in relation to such a God, it will be truly liberating in the world and in turn will be liberated from its own false and distorted forms.

This volume builds on an earlier inquiry in which I examined the relationship between evangelism and theology (Pickard 1993). However, it does not attempt to cover the full map of the theological territory relevant to a theology of evangelism. For example, there is no chapter on the "modern context(s)" for evangelism. Rather, at critical points in the discussion connections will be made with contemporary issues and questions in order to show how the proposals offered actually arise out of a critical engagement of the gospel with modern western society. A major area that deserves very careful attention in the light of this study is the issue of religious pluralism and its significance for evangelism. I hope to address this issue in the near future. Finally, this discussion does not seek to follow much of the current material on evangelism concerned for strategies, planning, and guided discussions of the how-to kind. There is much of value in the existing literature, and duplication is unnecessary. Instead, the present discussion is an attempt to identify some critical foundational issues in theology and church. It will try to show how renewed understanding in these areas provides a wider vision for contemporary evangelism. The intention of the present study has something of the character of a theological journey following the streams that flow from the hinterland of the contemporary church's evangelism. It us hoped that these explorations may prove worthwhile in identifying fresh springs to feed the gospel of God in the estuaries of our common life. We turn now to the first of the two main concerns of this volume, the relationship between evangelism and theology.

1

Evangelism and Theology: The Status of the Dialogue

But in your hearts set apart Christ as Lord. Always be prepared to give an answer to everyone who asks you to give the reason for the hope that you have. But do this with gentleness and respect.   — 1 Peter 3:15

An Uneasy Dialogue

What is the relationship between evangelism and theology? Do they, as suggested earlier, belong together and enrich each other, or are they essentially quite separate activities of the Christian community? And does it matter anyway? These questions form the backdrop for this and the following chapter.

Certainly, in the modern period of the Christian tradition we can observe, at a general level, an uneasy dialogue between evangelists and theologians — particularly those who belong to the field of systematics or dogmatic theology. They have not proved to be very compatible partners, the relationship having more the character of a stormy courtship ending in separation rather than a well-established marriage.

7

The nature of their partnership was well symbolized in August of 1960 when Billy Graham met Karl Barth — in Protestant circles arguably the two greatest figures in evangelism and theology, respectively, in the twentieth century. The Barthian interpretation of the meeting is recorded by Barth's biographer, Eberhard Busch (1976:446):

> [Barth's] son Markus brought them together in the Valais. However, this meeting was also a friendly one. "He's a 'jolly good fellow,' with whom one can talk easily and openly; one has the impression that he is even capable of listening, which is not always the case with such trumpeters of the gospel." Two weeks later Barth had the same good impression after a second meeting with Graham, this time at home in Basle. But, "it was very different when we went to hear him let loose in the St. Jacob stadium that same evening and witnessed his influence on the masses. I was quite horrified. He acted like a madman and what he presented was certainly not the gospel. It was the gospel at gunpoint....He preached the law, not a message to make one happy. He wanted to terrify people. Threats — they always make an impression. People would much rather be terrified than be pleased. The more one heats up hell for them, the more they come running." But even this success did not justify such preaching. It was illegitimate to make the gospel law or "to 'push' it like an article for sale. We must leave the good God freedom to do his own work."

It would, of course, be interesting to hear Graham's side of the meetings and his version of what happened at the St. Jacob stadium. At any rate, the story symbolizes something of the growing rift between theology and evangelism in the modern period. Thus William Abraham, in *The Logic of Evangelism* (1989:8f), notes the decline in the theological competence of the better-known evangelists over the generations. John Wesley was steeped in the classical Anglican theological tradition. Jonathan Edwards was not only a pastor and preacher involved in the "great awakening" of his time; he was also one of the great theologians of the modern Christian tradition. Charles Finney, though able intellectually, was less patient with the academy and more pragmatic in outlook. In later evangelists, such as D. L. Moody and Billy Sunday, little theological substance remains. Billy Graham, although sympathetic to the task of theology in the work of evangelism, has not been a significant contributor. The new generation of television evangelists have shown, in Abraham's view, little "serious attempt to reflect deeply about the work in which they are engaged" (:10). Lamenting this steady decline in the theological competence of evangelists over the generations and the problems associated with much modern mass evangelism, Abraham concludes that "it is not surprising if theologians prefer to pass by on the other side and leave the whole mess to whatever Samaritan may have mercy upon it" (ibid.). Yet, given the fortunes of theology in the wake of critical enlightenment thought — for example, the influence of rationalism and the loss of theological content; the tendency of theological discourse to legitimate rather than challenge prevailing social values — evangelists may have felt justified hurrying by a limping and ailing theology.

Evangelism and Theology: A Tale of Two Ships

Abraham's comments suggest, at first glance at least, that the old boundaries between evangelist and theologian are firmly in place. It might be said that the good ship *Evange-lism* has a lot of crew members, all busy at important tasks. But the ship is short of theological fuel. This fact remains hidden, at least to the upper-deck crew members. They do not know there is a shortage of fuel; they are not even aware that fuel of that kind is necessary. When they are not asleep, you can see them on deck painting, polishing, rearranging, and reorganizing. Meanwhile, down in the engine room the engineers are to be found. They meet regularly (code name "conferencing") to discuss the machinery of the ship and the latest navigational equipment. The question of fuel is an important topic on the agenda below deck. The problem is that the fuel supplied in the past no longer provides the energy the ship requires. What of course is desperately needed is new fuel, but where is it to come from?

So the good ship *Evangelism* is afloat, and its crew are highly activated, though if you look closely some appear a little worn. The really pressing issues about where the ship is headed, or rather how it is managing to head in a number of different directions, remain high on the agenda. But alas these matters do not seem to be any clearer for the many rounds of discussions held among engineers with occasional inputs from the above-deck crew. In fact, some crew members and a couple of engineers became so frustrated that they lowered a life raft and quietly paddled off to a desert island where they could learn again about building ships, ocean currents, and how to tread water over 70,000 fathoms. One day the crew on the deck of the good ship *Evangelism* noticed a very large ship passing by, *The Charismatic Queen*. The top decks were filled with people throwing streamers, waving, and beckoning the *Evangelism* crew to join them. It looked so inviting, even if, on closer inspection, the ship appeared to be going around in ever-decreasing circles.

It is important to note that there are other ships sailing upon this ecclesial ocean. The most impressive of these are the bulk oil tankers, in particular the 500,000-ton bulk carrier *Theological Tradition.* Oddly enough, when you inspect the various containers on such carriers you cannot find any, on first inspection at least, that would seem to provide the right kind of high octane fuel required for the good ship *Evangelism.* This, at least, was the opinion of some of the crew of the *Evangelism* ship who, upon sighting the bulk carrier *Theological Tradition* (a rare occurrence), rowed over to seek help with their fuel problem. Perhaps not surprisingly the crew were not well received. Captain Dogmatic was clearly embarrassed at the prospect of having to welcome the *Evangelism* crew. Following a clumsy and rather condescending greeting, the crew were allowed to sniff around. But not being at all sure of what they were looking for, they soon became discouraged and left. The Captain and crew of the tanker had tried to tell them that such carriers no longer serviced evangelism-class ships. In fact, it soon became apparent in the short exchange between the two crews that the tanker crew were no longer certain whom they supplied with fuel. But they were deeply committed to steaming around the ecclesial ocean, if only to meet up with other such tankers for cordial exchanges and perhaps the exchange of a container or two.

To be truthful, the tanker fleet was not in good shape. More ominously, there were moves afoot to remove the enormous tanker fleet to a safe harbor just off Cape Irrelevant. This would solve the immediate problem of harmful oil spills. In the last few decades, a number of dangerous ones had occurred that had caused a great deal of damage to the Evangelism-class ships. As a result, the tanker *Bultmann* had already been towed away to join the "Patristic Fleet." The tanker *Continental Calvin* and, alas, the giant tanker *Judicious Hooker,* much beloved of the tribe Anglicanus Classicus, had met a similar fate. Moreover, the H.M.S. *Higher Criticism* had long since rusted and been replaced by powerful and dangerous tankers from the shipyard "Postmodernism."

New Possibilities for Dialogue: A Brief Overview

Evangelists and theologians have, at least up until fairly recent decades, often seemed poles apart, unable and unwilling to come close, let alone join forces. A variety of reasons may account for this. Perhaps it is simply absence of interest in the concerns of each other. But this attitude may betray a deeper-rooted lack of conviction that either party needs the other or has anything to learn from the other. Furthermore, there is always the lurking fear that too close an association may result in compromise leading to loss of purity and eventual contamination. Often the theologian is frightened that the interchange will result in loss of academic and scholarly reputation. For their part, evangelists may feel that the academic labors of theologians yield little of value for the practical and urgent task of communicating the gospel. Alliance with the theologians might lead evangelists along unhelpful and pointless theological trails. However, the failure of the conversation between evangelists and theologians has led to a modern-day Babylonian captivity of the gospel. When evangelists and theologians regard each other with mutual suspicion and refuse to listen, challenge, and draw insights from each other, the communication of the gospel suffers and its liberating power cannot be experienced. Liberation thus begins with the Household of God; evangelism and theology require a freeing up for a fresh dialogue for the sake of the gospel. Such a dialogue is necessary if evangelism is to be freed from unhealthy and dubious practices and give faithful testimony to the gospel. For its part, theology requires such a dialogue in order to save it from fruitless abstraction and keep it focused on the gospel and the issues of contemporary society. As Wilbert Shenk notes: "Theology that is worked out as a community-building response to the contemporary situation will be lifegiving" (:72).

This seems to be the view of William Abraham, who recognizes the need for "a fresh universe of discourse that will open up a critical conversation on the complex issues that relate to evangelism" (:10). However, what this fresh approach might entail remains as yet undetermined. At one level there is no shortage of published material on evangelism as such, particularly over recent decades. Generally speaking, much of this material is preoccupied with questions of biblical foundations and principles, discussions concerned with apologetics, and the developing of effective programs for evangelism. The bibliographies of most books on evangelism will quickly bear this out (e.g., Green 1990; Kennedy 1972; Rainer 1989). In more recent material, greater attention to questions of culture and context can be discerned (e.g., Boff 1991; Costas 1989; Newbigin 1989).

Two dominant strands run through the material. One strand is associated with a strong focus on verbal proclamation and is characteristic of Protestant evangelicalism. Another strand has a strong emphasis on communicating the gospel through social action. This perspective has traditionally been an important plank in the World Council of Churches understanding of evangelism. However, these two strands are increasingly difficult to disentangle in Protestantism, particularly if statements from the Lausanne

Committee for World Evangelization and the WCC are to be taken with the seriousness they deserve. For example, both the Lausanne Committee's *Manila Manifesto* (1989) and the WCC *Evangelism and Mission: An Ecumenical Affirmation* (1982) indicate important attempts to develop an understanding of evangelism that includes both verbal proclamation and social action (see documents in Scherer and Bevans 1992). The traditional emphases remain, but the documents reflect the growing recognition that evangelism requires a proper interweaving of the words and deeds of the gospel. But is this sufficient? The rise of Pentecostalism in the twentieth century points to the fact that all the words and works in the world are of little value unless the evangelism pulse is driven by the Spirit of God (Pomerville 1985). Furthermore, the words and works of the gospel Spirit are ecclesial; they emerge from the life of the church and in turn create new communities of the gospel. This ecclesial orientation to evangelism, in which the concrete reality of the Christian community occupies a pivotal place as the primary agent in the communication the gospel, has become an increasingly important factor in the practice and theory of evangelism. This will be explored further in Chapter 4. However, at this stage we note that this strong ecclesial perspective and its link with the kingdom of God is a feature of important statements on the theology and practice of evangelism from the Roman Catholic and Orthodox churches (Scherer and Bevans 1992, pts. 2, 3). It seems that as we await the dawning of the third millennium the evangelism spectrum is becoming increasingly complex and interesting, a fact that can easily be confirmed by consulting the basic statements on mission and evangelism for the period 1974–91 compiled by James Scherer and Stephen Bevans.

The above developments suggest that the old boundaries between the churches are breaking down and the traditional standoff or disinterest between evangelist and theologian is beginning to change. Evangelism is moving in new directions and in this process seeks theology as a dialogue partner. What is required is a fresh willingness to listen and learn from each other, particularly those who see things differently but with whom is shared a common bond in communicating the mystery of the gospel. Indeed, it is the growing recognition of this common calling that is uniting evangelists and theologians. This is reflected in a rapidly increasing number of books on the theology of evangelism from particular ecclesial/theological traditions (e.g., Drummond 1992; Kolb 1984; Johnson 1987, 1991; Rainer 1989). Church history is being reinterpreted from an evangelistic perspective (Rudnick 1984). Reformed scholars are offering fresh interpretations of the Reformed tradition (Lovell 1990; Coalter and Cruz 1995), and within the Anglican tradition a fresh note on the subject can be discerned (Marshall 1990). There are vigorous and prophetic works calling the church to a new awareness of the importance of evangelism within the whole scheme of the liberation of the gospel (Pope-Levison 1991). In this latter regard, the writing of the Roman Catholic Leonardo Boff (1991) and the "holistic evangelism" of the Protestant Orlando Costas (1989) are important. However, their prophetic freshness at times slides into mere assertion; themes are presented but remain underdeveloped in relation to each other. Other important efforts remain, for the most part, within the field of biblical hermeneutics without venturing very far into the systematic task of theology (e.g., Arias and Johnson 1992). Some quite popular and influential material lacks any clear *theological* underpinning at all (Hunter 1992; McGavran 1988)

or, as in the case of Wimber (1985), requires further critical scrutiny. At a more popular level, Robert Coleman's
writings on evangelism (e.g., *The Master Plan of Evangelism* 1987 *Evangelism at the Cutting Edge* 1986) continue
to have a strong appeal, as do popular works in the vein of
Know and Tell the Gospel (1981) by the Australian evangelist John Chapman. The *Grove Booklets on Evangelism*
(1988–93) would seem to offer, in Western contexts, some
of the most intelligent, accessible, and practical approaches
to evangelism for the local church. Some recent books break
new ground and will have an important place in the ongoing conversation (Abraham 1989; Brueggemann 1993).
In a slightly more popular vein but full of good insights
are the works of Adams (1994), Drane (1994), and Fung
(1992). Jean-Pierre Jossua's autobiographical/theological reflection on the concept of the witness is an unusual and
insightful book that deserves more attention (Jossua 1985).

However, except for an opening chapter on theology and
evangelism by Abraham (1989) and Costas (1989), there is
little evidence that systematic theology (in contradistinction
from biblical, historical, and pastoral theology) has given
sustained attention to the subject of evangelism. Thus, although there are positive signs of a renewed dialogue, it is
not yet clear how systematic theology might contribute to a
new conceptuality with regard to evangelism or how this
discipline has been influenced by and benefited from the
evangelistic practices of the church.

Conclusion

This chapter has offered a brief overview of the state of the
dialogue between evangelism and theology. It seems that
there are signs of change and new possibilities for dialogue.

This dialogue will be mutually enriching and liberating for evangelism and theology only as the conversation continues and moves to deeper levels. This is not simply a practical matter; it is also a theological matter, for theology and evangelism share a common life-source. The church's practice of evangelism and theology arises out of its life in Christ. The common bond in Christ (Gal. 3:28) is thus the base from which theology and evangelism spring. The story of the bond we have in Christ is the story of the gospel, and the telling of the story is the communicative task of the Christian church. Evangelism and theology are woven together at their root, for they represent different but complementary efforts to communicate the gospel. Chapter 2 examines further the relationship between evangelism and theology by looking more closely at the theme of communication, an issue foundational for both activities of the church. The chapter will explore the centrality of communication and the problems and challenges that this raises for evangelism and theology.

2

Telling the Gospel Story:
A Question of Communication

How, then, can they call on the one they have not believed in? And how can they believe in the one of whom they have not heard? And how can they hear without someone preaching to them?   — Romans 10:14

The Priority of Communication

As suggested at the end of Chapter 1, both evangelism and theology are examples of the Christian community's communicative life. Accordingly, the purpose of this chapter is to offer a general framework for understanding communication in the Christian community. In particular, we will consider some of the contemporary problems and challenges to telling the gospel story with integrity and vitality. There is, of course, an urgent and practical issue at stake in the matter of communication: people cannot believe if they have not heard the message of the gospel (Rom. 10:14). Good communication thus lies at the heart of good evangelism and theology, and it is not surprising that the question of communication is on the evangelism agenda today (Babin 1991; Hunter 1992).

However, the question of communication is more than a practical task performed in order to convey information. Rather, it is a basic part of our human existence, even though its significance has not always been properly recognized. For example, its importance seems to be ignored in the seventeenth-century French philosopher René Descartes' famous maxim: "I think therefore I am." This approach to human existence has been foundational for Western thought and life but hardly does justice to the full complexity of what it means to be a human being. More recent approaches to the question have moved beyond the excessively individualist philosophy associated with Descartes and the Enlightenment tradition. In doing so they have stressed the social nature of human life and focused on the importance of communication as a fundamental feature of human life (McFadyen 1990). It is hard to ignore this newer perspective for the very good reason that "every act, every pause, every movement in living and social systems is also a message; silence is communication; short of death it is impossible for an organism or a person not to communicate" (Wilden 1980:124). It would seem that communication is both a *condition of* and *essential to* our humanity. Communication has been referred to as "the transmission of energy in a form" (Hardy and Ford 1984:157), a definition that points to the fact that communication cannot be restricted to language (that is, linguistic forms). Indeed, all language is communication, but very little communication is language. As Wilden notes, the "non-linguistic modes of communication in society include music, the visual arts, the visual aspects of film and television; kinship, status, money, sex and power, accent, height, shape and beauty; much mathematics, dreams, and fantasy; images, ideals, emotions, and desires; the production and exchange of commodities; and class, caste, race, and sex" (:137). Touch, for example, is a rich medium for communication. Visual communication is perhaps the richest of all. A traditional Chinese proverb states: "One hundred tellings are not as good as one seeing" (:122).

We often fail to recognize the importance and influence of other modes of communication, especially those associated with vision, movement, and the body. This failure is understandable given the tendency of Enlightenment rationalism to exalt language as "thought" or "reason" above other "modes of communication, such as the environment of non-verbal communication that makes thought and language possible" (ibid.:138). However, it is also the case that "there is no communication system between animals, insects, or computers that remotely approaches the complexity, flexibility, and capacities of language" (:136). We are more intimately involved in communication through language than in any other activity besides love and work, and both of these are modes of communication that usually require language. Communication is thus a general category within which language appears as a special case.

An important conclusion from these brief and unsurprising comments is that language is not simply a means to another end, an instrument for other purposes. Rather, language is a medium through which the communicative life occurs. In this sense it is constitutive of human life. Social life and personal identity are formed and shaped in relation to language. As such, language is a part of human reality rather than a copy or misrepresentation of it (:130).

Communication, the Church,
and the Word Tradition

These general remarks about communication and language are important in considering evangelism and theology in the church. Both these themes can be treated as *communicative tasks* of the church, and as such they can be done well or poorly. Accordingly, the main concern becomes the *improvement* of communication. This involves strengthening techniques and devising more appropriate strategies. In this context, evangelism can become preoccupied with strategic issues such as the principles of Jesus' evangelism and ways in which such methods can be effectively used in the church today (Coleman 1987).

This is all well and good, but it does not push the discussion very far. The main problem is that in this context communication is quickly reduced to questions of method and technique (Shenk 1995:97f). On this account communication is essentially a strategic matter — what the church has to do in order to "reach secular people" (Hunter 1992; Posterski 1989). Evangelism can assume a merely "instrumentalist" function and slide into a monological (i.e., one-way) discourse that becomes either manipulative or dominative. This approach is reductive and distortive of the gospel, which cannot be reduced to the delivery of certain information in a neat and pure form. Accordingly, advocates of an alternative view argue that good communication involves a self-giving that is more than merely information requiring a response. Rather, communication has the character of an open exchange in which the distance between hearer and speaker is bridged in a fulsome way that includes, but goes beyond, mere words. This presupposes a richer dialogical communication where the evangelist takes a gamble that in the interchange all participants will be challenged and undergo change. Yet even in this more open and risky wager on the gospel, communication remains a primarily strategic, task-orientated activity.

Communication moves to a different level when it is no longer considered as simply one task among many but becomes a way of understanding the whole life of the church (Baum and Greeley 1974). From this perspective, communication is not so much a task of the church but concerns its very existence. The focus is on the church as a communicative system with a primary concern on the quality of interactions that occur between texts, traditions, persons, and institutions. This approach to communication offers important insights into the structuring and activities of ecclesial life. It also exposes the operation of ideological elements that distort and disrupt communication of the gospel. This raises questions of an ethical kind that will be discussed later in this chapter. For the moment we note that, at its deepest theological level, this approach provides the basis for an understanding of the church as a "sacrament of nondominative communication" (:92, 98) or, more positively, an open, dialogical community. The critical factor is the quality of the church's communicative life. It will be high quality to the extent that it mirrors the character of God and thus intends to be a community of open and free — that is, nondominative — communication.

Sadly, it is simply a fact that the ideal of open, dialogical communication has not always been respected and achieved in the life of the church. This is particularly so in evangelism and theology where the primary medium of communication — that is, word — has often silenced other voices in the conversation of the gospel with the world. However, the context for such domination by word communication is much more complex at the end of the twentieth century. Today religious communication is heavily influenced by visual and electronic media; there is no longer one dominant scheme of communication. Rather, religious communication operates through a variety of mediums including language, affinity (involving relationships, friendship and spirit), social groups (the poor — the conscience of the church), and aesthetics (Babin 1991:chap. 4).

Yet the long tradition in Christianity of "wording" the gospel persists. At one level this is not surprising. It has to do with the character of God, whose word is creative of light and life, whose word takes the form of Torah for the people of Israel, and whose word is spoken by the prophets. This domain of *logos* communication comes to its most concentrated form in Jesus Christ: "In the beginning was the Word, and the Word was with God, and the Word was God.... The Word became flesh and lived for awhile among us" (John 1:1, 14). It is the word of God that is preached in the early church, and the word of God expands in its reach and penetration (Acts 6:7; 12:24). The subsequent Christian theological tradition represents a sustained attempt to give voice to the *logos* of the gospel, and in the domain of theology and evangelism communication through word will always be significant. However, precisely because this *logos* tradition in Christianity has often operated in a dominating way, today we face a crisis in communication through the word, a crisis that has direct impact on evangelism and theology.

The Crisis in Word Communication

The crisis in linguistically ordered communication has been gathering momentum for some time. In everyday discourse, language is somewhat of a debased currency — the rhetoric of "political-speak" fueling popular suspicions that words often conceal the hollowness, meaninglessness, and ignorance of our times. This is unsurprising, given the social fragmentation and attendant uncertainties and mistrusts that beset modern culture (Giddens 1990). Under such conditions, the temptation to deploy language to mask our anxieties and cover our inadequacies is almost irresistible. To what then does language refer? One result of the debasement of language is that words lose their meaning and potency; the form of language remains, but the content seems to evaporate.

The problem of the relation between language and reality is even more acute in theology. Here, for example, the notion of a world created and rationally ordered according to the divine *logos* (John 1:1ff) is challenged by postmodernist approaches that tend to highlight the fragmented and chaotic nature of human existence. In doing so they raise suspicions about any attempt to make connections between the particulars of our life that point to a larger and more comprehensive reality derived from and sustained by the *logos* of God (Taylor 1984:52–68). This general critique of *logos* reality is aligned to the emergence of feminist critiques of Christianity's oppressive patriarchal structure and its undergirding logocentricism (Chopp 1991:1–39). A further challenge to the emphasis on the "word" tradition in Christianity arises from the religious pluralism of today's global village. Christianity has to reckon with the fact that other traditions such as Hinduism and Buddhism do not seem to require a notion of *logos* in order to understand and explain the structure of the world (Kelly 1989:234ff).

Such critiques go right to the core of a Christian tradition that has struggled over the last couple of centuries against erosion of belief and a more general loss of confidence that God is really present in the Christian community. Uncertainties in this regard fuel the suspicion that the language of faith no longer witnesses to a transcendent reality but is purely descriptive of the phenomena of ecclesial life (Farley 1975:6–23). In this context, religious language is accorded a secondary significance — a medium for expressing something more primal in human experience. In theology this means that language functions to express feelings, attitudes, existential orientations and practices rather than what happens at the level of "symbolic objectifications" of realities beyond the domain of personal experience (Lindbeck 1984:17). The danger is that religious language can become caught in the trap of human subjectivity. It becomes unclear how human words mirror or refer to the God of Christian faith. Evangelism can be reduced to the good news *of my life* rather than the good news of the life of God in which I live. Theological discourse might end up being *just what I think;* believing in God might become "believing in believing in God" (Farley 1975:15). On this account, our religious language becomes almost a private language with little capacity to connect with others.

An alternative approach to the subjectivism of the above is a strong objectivist position. In this case it is assumed that the words we use correspond to reality both human and divine. It is assumed that there is only one way to express the truth of faith. This is exemplified in modern theology by a form of doctrinalism that codifies truth in particular and fixed language forms. This form of propositional objectivity ends up codifying God, a point well appreciated by Karl Barth who argued that the codification of belief into certain articles of faith — as occurred in Protestant Scholasticism of the seventeenth century — and the subsequent raising of such articles to the status of a "classic text" involved "a definition, limitation and restriction of the Word of God" (Barth 1956a:865). When the expression in doctrine of the church's encounter with "God in His Word" became the pretext for "the establishment of specific, irrevocable, fundamental articles" (:864), then the way was blocked, in Barth's view, for the free operation of the Word of God and the church. Barth correctly diagnosed the mistake here; human words ceased to be guided by God's Word but rather blocked the full and free-flowing Divine Word. The dynamic of Christian dogmatics was undermined. Nevertheless, under conditions of social instability and fragmentation, and with widespread loss of confidence in the sufficiency of God for the affairs of the world, attempts to secure tighter institutional controls upon the language of faith exercise a strong appeal. In this theological reductionism, full and free speech is thwarted in the interests of a false notion of purity which requires a tight one-to-one correspondence between the reality that faith witnesses to and its form in language.

Anxiety over the crisis in word communication has contributed to an evangelism and theology that is often sterile, predictable, and uninviting. This is evident both in a tight, formalized reductionism — a feature of religious fundamentalism — and in an undisciplined subjectivizing of faith. Neither approach seems to be generated out of basic Christian praise of God. This reference is either lacking or at best only indirectly intended. This is not surprising, given the emphasis on either getting the language exactly correct or preoccupation with the experience of the self. Yet the Christian gospel points us in another direction — to the God who gives joy-filled responses: to the God who, in the Christian tradition, authorizes and legitimates free-flowing, abundant speech. This was epitomized in the experience of Pentecost in the early church (Acts 2ff). What was remarkable about this new and surprising telling of the good things of God was that both speaker and hearer were changed and freed for a new way of living, thinking, and being. The history of the Christian tradition from that early Pentecost points to the new life of freedom and joy that comes from God and is repeatedly offered back to God in praise and service. When faith in God is driven by this dynamic and overflows into Christian witness through evangelism and theology, the result is liberation: "It is for freedom that Christ has set us free" (Gal. 5:1). This is a quite different way of understanding communication through word when compared with the subjectivist and objectivist approaches referred to above. Its implications for the church's communication in evangelism and theology are examined in the following chapter. However, it is important first to examine the ethical issues for evangelism that arise from the crisis in word communication.

Communicating with Integrity:
The Ethical Challenge

Within the contemporary context of the debasement of language, where the spoken and written word is regularly used to manipulate others and market goods of little real value, a question arises for the Christian community about the ethics of its own communication. This is particularly relevant to the ethics of its evangelism that, on any account, includes an element of persuasion. This is clearly the case in more fundamentalist approaches to evangelism, though it is not absent in any telling of the good news, at least insofar as a hope is entertained that the story being told may be found convincing and worthy of embrace. When does such communication become manipulative and coercive? Or is it the case that all attempts to influence others are flawed from the outset? Some Christians might raise a question as to whether evangelism is ethical at all. My own view is that this would be a difficult position to sustain in the light of the way the Christian gospel actually works: It is essentially good news, a story worth telling and living and inviting others to share in. The more pressing issue is how the story is told and lived. Perhaps it is not so much a question about whether evangelism is ethical or not but rather, what is an appropriate ethic for evangelism?

This question takes the crisis in word communication to a deeper level and involves the Christian church in an ethical challenge of major proportions. Specifically, it requires this community to find a way of communicating the gospel with integrity. To have integrity is to have a certain wholeness, uprightness, and purity of life. It applies not only to individuals but also to communities and identifies something of their fundamental character and the values that inform and guide their life. When integrity is a mark of the Christian community, it will be evident not only in its communication with others but in the way it actually gives integrity to those with whom it engages. This issue is critical for the church's evangelism that easily succumbs to the discourse of Western capitalism with its focus on efficiency, effectiveness, and results (productivity) and in so doing turns the "other" into an object or commodity. The basic problem with this approach to economic life and by extension the witness of the church to the gospel is brought out clearly and sharply in the analysis of modernity offered by the philosopher Jürgen Habermas. His "critical theory of society" (Geuss 1981) provides a helpful framework for our discussion of the ethics of evangelism and clarifies what communicating with integrity might involve.

At the center of Habermas's discussion of modern culture is his concern for communication that promotes genuine understanding between peoples. This is what he terms "ideal communication," and it is developed in detail in his theory of "communicative action" (Habermas 1984:273–337). In this respect he has already proved an important dialogue partner with theologians (Browning and Fiorenza 1992) and, in particular, those concerned with the life of the Church and its communication (Lakeland 1990; cf. Mudge 1992:195–210).

In discussing communication Habermas focuses on what he terms "strategic action" (:285ff). This is action "orientated to success," and the priority here is "effectiveness." Strategic action can occur in a number of forms of which the most dangerous and common is what Habermas calls *concealed* strategic action. Such action operates as either *conscious* deception or *unconscious* deception, otherwise known as "systematically distorted communication" (:332ff). The notion of "systematically distorted communication" is critical for Habermas, and, as we will see below, it has important implications for the church's communication of the gospel. Systematically distorted communication is explained by Habermas with reference to the Freudian theory of the unconscious. In this theory repression of conflicts is explained in terms of human defense mechanisms. The value of Habermas's analysis is that he is able to show how the Freudian theory of repression "leads to disturbances of communication on both the intrapsychic and *interpersonal* levels" (:332; my italics). The result is that strategic actions have only "the appearance of communicative action," that is, of seeking genuine understanding. In fact one, of the parties in the interaction fails to recognize (self-deceived) that his or her action is really orientated to success (effectiveness) rather than genuine understanding via freely arrived-at consensus. The distortion in communication is unintended and thus systemic.

Habermas's discussion is of particular relevance for the church. It is reasonable to think that any human community that tries to respect the humanity of its constituents (such as the church) will reject all forms of manipulation (conscious deception) and strive to rid itself of all forms of systematically distorted communication (unconscious deception). Yet, as Habermas recognizes, overcoming systematically distorted communication is very difficult, for the distortions are subliminal and usually go unnoticed. Accordingly, a chief aim of a *critical* theory of society is to uncover such distortions and thus facilitate social and personal liberation. However, as the theologian Paul Lakeland notes: "Like any therapeutic mechanism . . . its efficacy depends on a willingness on the part of the subject to recognize in at least some initial way the need for healing" (:107). Yet this is a problem for the church precisely because it operates self-consciously under a mandate from God to be a community that proclaims the good news of liberation to the world. Although the failings of particular individuals and the occasional distortions that have erupted in its history might well be accepted — it is, after all, made up of ordinary mortals — it is exceedingly difficult for the church to recognize that "it could be victimized by a variety of unconscious deception, since that weakness would go to the roots of the whole society, rather that be placed on the shoulders of sinful individuals" (:108). Lakeland writes as a Roman Catholic and singles out, as a special example of systematically distorted communication, the sexism of his own communion.

Sexism, of course, is not confined to the Roman Catholic communion. It can be found within the communicative paradigms of evangelism and theology in most churches. After all, who has traditionally written the books in these areas? The situation is changing, though much more critical work needs to be done to examine the impact of feminism on the character, discourse, and practices of contemporary evangelism and the progress that is being made in overcoming systematically distorted communication. The issue has been sharply put in a recent monograph, *Gossiping the Gospel: Women Reflect on Evangelism:* "An emphasis on evangelism has often meant a movement away from those trends in the church which have affirmed and listened to women, an emphasis on individual faith and salvation rather than concern about justice making, peace and the environment, and towards growth in the church rather than the active presence of the church in the community" (Neave 1992:1). The essays in this book creatively explore new ways of evangelism in the light of women's experiences of the gospel. In doing so the book uncovers and critiques the unconscious distortions in the prevailing evangelism traditions of the Christian churches.

However, as noted above, strategic action occurs in a number of forms. Concealed strategic action that is systematically distorted is only one form. There is also, and more positively, what Habermas calls "open strategic action." This identifies action that has been *openly agreed upon and embraced by the community.* Evangelism might well fall into this category of open strategic action orientated to success, where success is defined as "the appearance in the world of a desired state, which can, in a given situation, be causally produced through goal-orientated action or omission" (Habermas 1994:285). Indeed, the vocation of the Christian community to be a sharer of the good news would seem to be quite fundamental to its identity, regardless of the many different ways in which this communicative activity is construed. Accordingly, "evangelization is a paradigmatic example of 'action orientated to success,' if being the Church God intended is taken to be being successful" (Lakeland 1990:110). Yet, as Lakeland notes, "success" or "effectiveness" in evangelism is "measured by conformity to the divine intent," and this will necessarily require the church to have a clear understanding about "what God's mission for the church is" (ibid.). Only when the church has clarity in this regard will it be able to differentiate between appropriate and inappropriate strategic action. On this account the character of the Christian God and the nature of the ecclesial community that worships this God provide the broader horizon and critical perspective for the many acts of communication that make up the evangelistic practices of the church.

Being clear about God's mission for the church is, therefore, the real challenge. This involves the Christian community in a quest for understanding that goes beyond strategic actions that are success driven, as is often the case in evangelism. Only when there is an attempt to reach genuine understanding is there, in Habermas's sense, true "communicative action." The point is that in genuine communicative action "participants are not primarily orientated to their own individual successes" (Habermas:286). The orientation to reach understanding — in this case God's mission for the church — involves a community's fundamental concern for truth, both in its expression of its own identity and more general states of affairs, and an effort to determine the rightness of the norms governing interpersonal interactions of the community. This impulse within the Christian community to a deeper understanding of its identity and task is part of a continuous critical process. Ideally this quest is equally shared in by all; the intention is to seek consensus; the appropriate stance is one of openness to new insight and revisions; and the presupposition is that the process of reaching understanding occurs as shared conversations find embodiment in practices appropriate for the community. Only under such conditions is there genuinely "communicative action" (:286–95). Lakeland's conclusion is critical: "The question of appropriateness becomes one of determining what strategic action respects the character of a community orientated to understanding" (:111). Thus, although we might fully endorse the fact that evangelism is an appropriate strategic action for the church, such action must respect the communicative character of the God to whom the church offers its praise. Under these conditions the drive for "effective" evangelism gives way to "faithful" evangelism that is guided by the character of the God exemplified in the life and teachings of Jesus. Faithfulness thus involves a double reference to both the content of the Christian story and the manner in which this story is lived out with others in the world. The gospel is good news but only insofar as it is expressed in a way that embodies goodness toward others. This will be the mark of the church's communicative integrity.

Much of the history of the church is a story of struggle to embody such integrity in its communication of the gospel. A key challenge has been to bring its many strategic actions into line with its fundamental character as a community of "good news." For example, Paul's letter to the church at Galatia points to the struggle that particular community had to live out the freedom appropriate for those who were no longer "slaves" but sons and daughters of God (Gal. 4:7). Modern biblical scholarship has highlighted the difficult challenges and tensions faced in the Christian communities as they sought to live the gospel in differing contexts. What was deemed good news had to be sensitively and courageously expressed in a manner appropriate to local conditions. Recent work on the gospel communities has important implications and insights for contemporary evangelistic practices, the forms they might take, and the challenges they must grapple with (see, e.g., Crosby 1988, on questions of gospel and justice in the Matthean community; and Brown 1979, on the Johannine communities). For example, Brown (:59–91) identifies a major tension in the Johannine community. On the one hand, he identifies those advocates of retreat from the world — a response born of disappointment at the poor reception and even rejection of the gospel. On the other hand, he refers to those who found in the gospel (John 3:16) new resources and motivations to move out into the world (John 20:21). In the former view, evangelism essentially operates as a foray into an alien environment with the intention of incorporating people into a closed, sectlike community. In the latter view, there is potential for a far more open and positive engagement of the gospel with society. The Johannine example indicates that it is the fundamental self-understanding of the Christian community that sets the parameters within which the character and ethic of evangelism takes place.

This discussion points to the importance of reconnecting evangelism with the values and character of the Christian community, in particular those values and orientations that embody God's loving and arresting presence in the midst of the world rather than apart from it. It is a sad fact that gospel communication has often lost its moorings with the Christian community. Although the strategic action may remain *open* — that is, agreed upon by the community — at least to some significant degree it is often embodied in practices that only partially at best reflect the true gospel character of the community. The litmus test of this occurs when strategic action shifts from an appropriate action *of* humans to an action *upon* humans. In this case such action lacks a communicative integrity; it is unable to give integrity to others, nor can it foster true freedom in the Spirit. When evangelism operates in this manner, it indicates that it is no longer operating under the constraints of the inner ideals of the Christian community — that is, the ideal of nondominative communication exemplified in the life of Jesus. Conditions emerge wherein the strategic action becomes concealed, either consciously — that is, manipulation of others on the basis that the ends justify the means — or unconsciously, the result being systematically distorted communication. The negative impact such distortions can have on communication can often be traced to a quite defective understanding of what Christianity is all about. This could occur, for example, when the God of the gospel is resolved into a being who has made laws and punishes those who continue in rebellious transgression of such laws. In this case God's love is ultimately subsumed under God's wrath, with severe implications for the interpretation of the passion and death of Christ and the dynamics of God's *conditional* mercy. In this instance a defective construal of Christianity creeps in unrecognized, as it were, and legitimates evangelistic practices more in accord with actions done to (upon) others rather than with and for them. This suggests that where the nature of the communicative community has been misunderstood, ignored, or distorted, albeit unintentionally, visions of "success" or "effectiveness" become driven by the undertow of ideological forces, and communication is instrumentalized. The practical result is that face-to-face relations are no longer directed to the fostering of understanding, and the "other" quickly becomes a potential consumer or "object" and is accordingly "colonized." Clearly, the "other" can be an individual, a community, or a larger national grouping, as the history of evangelization indicates.

An Ethic of Vulnerability

In terms of the above discussion, it is clear that good evangelism and theology involves more than finding the most effective strategic action or pure and correct forms of words. Rather, it requires a proper appreciation of the church as a communicative community where the ideal of nondominative communication orders its life. The apostle Paul was well aware of this inescapable *ethical* dimension to communication of the gospel and the danger of manipulation and misuse of power. Thus he reminded the Christian community at Corinth: "For I resolved to know nothing while I was with you except Jesus Christ and him crucified. I came to you in weakness and fear, and with much trembling. My message and preaching were not with wise and persuasive words, but with a demonstration of the Spirit's power, so that your faith might not rest on [human] wisdom, but on God's power" (1 Cor. 2:2–5). This paradox at the heart of Christianity is at the heart of a faithful evangelizing ethic. It points to the fact that when communication of the gospel is informed by the nondominative ideal, God's power is manifest through what appears as weakness (2 Cor. 4:7). This communicative ethic of vulnerability is developed in the contemporary secular sphere by Habermas when he extols the virtues of open, rational conversation among free and equal people. Whether this is possible is a controversial matter. Many events in our contemporary world would seem to suggest that Habermas's proposal is more of a pipe dream, though the notion of ideal communication does provide "a critical perspective and an emancipatory energy in political life" (Mudge 1992:198) and thus is a useful means to evaluate the church's communicative efforts.

A question arises, however, concerning the conditions that would justify and sustain such communicative endeavors. Habermas ignores or rather discounts the importance of religious underpinnings at this point. In fact, it is difficult to see what foundation he has left save for rationality itself (Hardy 1989:28). Yet the question implicit here is critical: What sort of community could embody such ideals for open and free communication, cope with repeated failure and disappointment, and foster genuine hope for the future of human society and creation? Minimally, it would have to be a community marked by inner integrity and therefore a respect and care for all with whom it communicates. This is a major ethical challenge for the church today as it seeks to share the gospel story. How the church handles this challenge will determine how well it is able to respond creatively to the crisis in communication today.

Conclusion

The purpose of the present chapter has been to provide a general introduction to communication and its relationship to evangelism and theology. With this in mind we have considered three things: (1) the importance of communication in society and the church; (2) the contemporary crisis in word communication and its impact on the Christian community's witness to the gospel: (3) the ethical challenge for the church's evangelism posed by the wider problems associated with communication through word today. A general framework has thus been provided in which to explore, in the following chapter, the relationship between evangelism and theology in the communication of the gospel. Specifically, the concern of Chapter 3 is the dynamics of communication with respect to evangelism and theology, and the importance of their complementary relationship for the vitality of the church's gospel.

3

The Dynamics of
Gospel Communication

Pray also for me, that whenever I open my mouth, words may
be given me so that I will fearlessly make known the mystery
of the gospel.   — Ephesians 6:19

Communicating the Gospel:
A Theological Exploration

This Pauline request is multilayered. It includes the calling and responsibility felt by the writer to find words for
the Word, the appeal for prayer from other Christians, the
richness of the gospel, and the accompanying sense that
new contexts and circumstances require fresh proclamation.
How does this all work? Is it sufficient simply to appeal to
the Holy Spirit to sort it all out? Certainly, the agency of
the Spirit is at the heart of this request. Yet an equally important issue concerns how human beings participate with
the Spirit in finding the right words for the "mystery of
the gospel." How is it that our speech is not held back
but released in order to praise God? Such questions point
to the need in the church for an improved understanding

of the dynamics of full and free communication. This is a theological issue that does not usually receive much attention. It is essentially an issue to do with the theological processes at work in the effort to communicate the gospel. The theologian thus asks the questions: What happens in good communication of the gospel? How do the activities of evangelism and theology faithfully reflect the God to whom they bear witness? By what means can a full and free communication of the gospel be achieved? Under what conditions could systematically distorted communication, as discussed in the previous chapter, be disclosed and genuine emancipation occur? How might evangelism and theology be understood as complementary activities necessary for the sustainability of the gospel?

The theologian asks these questions in order to uncover the inner dynamics and processes that drive gospel communication. The discussion proceeds on the assumption that a better understanding of these processes as they relate to evangelism and theology will contribute to a more confident and vital telling of the gospel story.

This chapter examines three key features of communication in evangelism and theology that are necessary for full and free articulation of the gospel. First, full and free speech involves an implicit appeal to simplicity. Second, such communication operates with a bias toward repetition. Third, it witnesses to the presence of wisdom. Within each of these three dimensions of communication, evangelism and theology operate in different but complementary and enriching ways. A consideration of these three elements of good communication leads into a brief discussion of the purpose of communication and the character of the Divine agent in this activity of the church.

The Appeal to Simplicity

The first mark of full and free communication is simplicity. The contemporary Protestant theologian Jürgen Moltmann has said: "What cannot be said simply does not need to be written at all. Simplicity is the highest challenge to Christian theology. Theology stands under the demand to speak simply because, as Christian theology, it stands or falls with the church" (1978:9). In the context, Moltmann clearly has in mind the issue of communication in the church. His sentiments would, no doubt, find joyful approval among those involved in evangelism. Before we go any further, however, it is also well to note that for every difficult and complex problem there is always a perfectly reasonable and simple answer that is wrong!

Nevertheless, the good news is never confusing or complicated. Neither is it simplistic. There is, it seems, a way of wording the faith that communicates with a profound simplicity the mystery of the gospel. Such simplicity is not that which "boils" truth down to the bare essentials, though we should note that the search for the essence of Christianity has a long and important history in Protestantism (Sykes 1984). It is a wholly understandable strategy and has its appeal both in theology and evangelism. It can lead to the supposition of the simplicity of the gospel, which, in an important sense, is absolutely vital to retain (Kerr 1991:1–10). In this case simplicity is a corollary of that childlike faith that Jesus enjoined upon adults: "Unless you change and become like little children you will never enter the kingdom of heaven" (Matt. 18:3). However, the "simplicity" strategy can easily lead to a "checklist" gospel in which certain propositions are offered for assent.

But there is a way of communicating with simplicity that

does not sacrifice depth and profundity but rather manages to compress it into brief form. Poetry at its best exemplifies this form of communication. For the evangelist the simple but profound message might take the form of a "word in season" — that word for which the writer of the letter to the Ephesians prays: "Pray also for me, that whenever I open my mouth, words may be given me so that I will fearlessly make known the mystery of the gospel" (Eph. 6:19). This prayer is not a request for "the bare essentials" but a compelling snapshot of the faith of Jesus Christ, a rich compression of the truth. It is precisely because the gospel is not simple but profound that the prayer is for wisdom to express the mystery with simplicity. There are no blueprints for achieving this simple profundity in the truth. Sharpness, clarity, and depth of insight are not merely well-honed skills but capacities bestowed by God for his praise. Furthermore, in the body of Christ it should not be presumed that all these qualities will be present in the same person to the same degree. What is critical is an openness to God in order that utterance may be given the evangelist as he or she begins to speak, so that he or she may be freely released to open up the secrets of the good news of God. In doing so, the evangelist offers a highly compressed statement of the faith — the whole in a little. Furthermore, there is no appeal here to a ready-made plan. Rather, what we find is a reliance upon God as one speaks freely and flowingly of the love of God in Christ Jesus. As the Ephesians passage makes clear, this activity is Spirit-led, informed by the love of Christ, propelled through prayer, and reliant upon the intercession of the Christian community. It thus involves an inescapable human dimension.

I have suggested that simplicity, properly understood, is not reductive of the gospel but rather is a way of gathering its richness and profundity into a brief and concentrated form. This is the kind of simplicity appropriate to the fullness of God witnessed to in the gospel. However, precisely because the evangel is *this* kind of simplicity it is capable of significant extension. Indeed, there is a sense in which the Christian gospel has an inbuilt drive for extension. The image that most readily comes to mind here is the piano accordion, which requires successive movements of compression and extension as it makes its music. Similarly, this constant movement from compression to extension in a free-flowing way belongs to "the mystery of the gospel." Within this dynamic of gospel communication, evangelism represents a *recurring moment*. It has a critical part to play in the process of communication, but it has more of the character of comma rather than a full stop.

By contrast, theological discourse participates in this communication process as it moves beyond the comma, unraveling the gospel further, bringing fresh illumination and sharpness to it. In this sense theological discourse is called to extend playfully and joyfully the truth as it is in Jesus. A good example of this dynamic between compression and systematic extension of faith is provided by the theologian Paul Tillich. Tillich recognized the importance of simplicity in the gospel in relation to his own highly developed systematic enterprise: "The statement that Jesus is the Christ contains in some way the whole theological system, as the telling of a parable of Jesus contains all artistic potentialities of Christianity" (1968:215).

When simplicity is reconceived as concentration of richness and profundity, evangelism and theology can be understood as *complementary forms of gospel communication*. Evangelism represents a concentration point (the comma in the sentence); theology represents the extended form of communication. Good communication requires both compressed and extended discourse. Evangelism and theology act as catalysts for each other in the process of communication, and what we discover is a dynamic relationship between the two. The free-flowing communication of theological discourse is continually refocused and concentrated by the evangelist, whose task is to tell the story of the gospel with a fresh and arresting simplicity. Compression of the gospel in a concentrated form, as in evangelism, is thus a recurring moment in the communicative dynamic of the Christian faith. Accordingly, in terms of the dynamics of communication, evangelism and theology exhibit a fundamental complementarity. Furthermore, recognition of the character of evangelism as a *recurring* moment in the church's communicative activity suggests a second feature of gospel communication that might be termed the bias toward repetition.

The Bias Towards Repetition

Repetition is not usually treated as a theme in modern theology, although it is important in everyday life and thought, and certainly warrants serious theological consideration. Good evangelism evidences certain recurring patterns or references to God's ways with this world and human life. The history of the Christian tradition is informed by a recurring focus on the creative, redemptive, and life-giving character of the triune God. This is the God who is praised in Jesus Christ. On this account, evangelism might be understood "as the horizontal dimension of praise *repeated* and *explained* to others so they can join the community of praise" (Hardy and Ford 1994:19; my italics). From this perspective it is not the fact of repetition per se but its quality that is of critical importance.

Repetition in evangelism and in everyday life has both healthy, energizing forms as well as more disturbed, barren, and ultimately destructive forms. Modern society is highly repetitive in its structure and routine. Negative forms of repetition abound. For many, the world of heavy industry and the office computer is one of repetitive and unfulfilling work practices where human beings often function in a machinelike manner. In the area of mental health, the compulsion to endlessly repeat certain behavior patterns is well known. Again, the loss of the power of recall in Alzheimer's disease means that those who love and care for such people are locked into repetitive communication patterns.

In modern society, repetition is viewed negatively, as counterproductive if not destructive to the development of personal life. In this context, repetition is often equated with inauthenticity. Lionel Trilling puts the matter sharply: "In an increasingly urban and technological society, the natural processes of human existence have acquired a moral status in the degree that they are thwarted" (quoted in Sykes 1984:325). Commenting on this, the theologian Stephen Sykes states: "Anything resembling a mechanical process, and that would include the order and repetition of a liturgy, is felt to be inimical to the authenticity of experience and being" (ibid.). The drive in society for constant change, the discarding of items and ideas from the past and present, and the quest for the totally new is both powerful, controversial, and difficult to sustain. Advertising is a good example of this search to overcome repetition. It is, of course, a self-defeating exercise, because maximum exposure of the consumer public to the new product is paramount; yet such exposure requires repetition, and so the cycle is perpetuated.

The negative aspects of repetition ought not blind us to the fact that repetition is an important and necessary feature of our everyday life. If the toothbrush and soap as well as a regular and balanced food intake are to count, it is obvious that the repetition of the daily rituals associated with these things gives vitality and freshness to human life. Definite recurring patterns of behavior, communication, and exchange, such as greetings and farewells seem to be a necessary part of the healthy ordering of human society.

Not surprisingly, the positive and negative aspects of repetition can be discerned in religious life, including its worship. For example, Anglican worship has traditionally been patterned liturgically around the *Book of Common Prayer.* As the title indicates, it was prayer that was common to the congregation and repeated Sunday by Sunday and daily for those who said the Daily Offices. At the opposite end of the spectrum is Pentecostalism, whose church life is self-consciously nonliturgical, seeking freedom and spontaneity. In between are a whole range of differing ecclesial traditions. How is repetition relevant here? It is relatively commonplace to view more structured liturgical forms as unhelpfully repetitive over against more free-flowing, charismatic worship. However, highly structured worship does have the capacity to generate freedom. One is mercifully relieved from the trap of human subjectivity fixated on its own condition. Freshness from the transcendent presence of God becomes a real possibility. But of course it is also true that such worship can prove sleep inducing. At the other end of the spectrum, Pentecostal worship can assume a highly predictable and structured form in which the weekly repetition of certain activities is eagerly sought among the gathered worshipers. Music in worship is undergoing a renaissance right now. One feature of the newer forms of music is repetition. This has the capacity to completely kill the spirit or alternatively take it to new heights. It is not repetition per se that is the problem but its quality, that is, whether or not it mediates freshness.

Accordingly, there is an expectation in evangelism that what is proclaimed today is the same good news that brought redemption yesterday and will do so tomorrow. Minimally, we are right to expect a recurring pattern in the proclamation of the evangel. Furthermore, earlier it was suggested that this recurring pattern will have a Trinitarian form if it is to do justice to God's relation with creation. In this sense, certain elements of the evangel will recur: creation, redemption, fulfillment. These elements will be developed in relation to Jesus and the Spirit. The challenge is to repeat the "evangel" in its fullness — its rich simplicity — rather than some mutilated form. There is, at this level, good and bad evangelism.

Theological discourse participates in the dynamic of creative repetition. Here the aim is comprehensive communication of the truth of Christianity. So what ought to emerge in good theology is a full opening of the gospel as it is woven into myriad themes and life situations. Furthermore, what we ought to observe and in fact can discern in the Christian tradition is a recurring engagement with a Trinitarian understanding of God. Why Trinitarian? Because this is the form of the God who has generated Christian worship, mission, and service in history. A recurring Trinitarian pattern in theology can, of course, be linked to the very nature of the being of God. This was articulated most powerfully in the twentieth century by Karl Barth, who referred to a threefold "repetition in God" (1975:366), a repetition that was highly sophisticated and programmatic for his theological enterprise. Accordingly, what is revealed and witnessed to in Scripture is a three-fold differentiation of God in an unimpaired unity (:299). A repetition of God occurs in three quite "inexchangeable" modes of being: "God reveals Himself [*sic*]. He reveals Himself through Himself. He reveals Himself . . . this sub-ject, God, the Revealer, is identical with his act in revelation and also identical with its effect" (:296). For this reason the doctrine of revelation begins with the doctrine of the triune God. In Barth's theory of the repetition of God, priority tends to be given to the unity rather than the threefoldness within God. His tendency to modalism is recognized by a recent commentator: "God's triple restoration of himself is much more prominent than his relation to himself" (Heron 1983:167). Yet Barth, like many before and after him, was struggling to do justice to the God revealed in Jesus and the Spirit. This Jesus of Nazareth lived in relation to, but differ-entiated from, both his Abba God and the Spirit/Paraclete. How this distinction yet unity within the Divine life could be properly accounted for has been a critical issue in the church. In this context the notion of God's threefold rep-etition as Father, Son, and Spirit has provided a powerful and compelling means of articulating the biblical witness to God's revelation. From this perspective it seems that some notion of repetition belongs to the dynamic of the being of God revealed in the gospel. In other words, creative repeti-tion is not simply a convenient strategy for the evangelist or theologian to gain attention or make a point. Rather, it is a dynamic that reaches back into the very character of the God of the Christian gospel.

However, it is precisely at this point that the problem of repetition becomes acute. Good repetition requires *freshness through sameness*. Certainly, this was the burden of Barth's development of the threefold repetition in God: "Although, in keeping with God's riches, revelation is never the same but always new, nevertheless, as such it is always in all circumstances the promulgation of the logos, of the Lordship of God" (1975:306). What is required in good evangelism and theology is creative repetition. This will involve a continual interpretive effort that will be more or less successful to the extent that it offers a faithful contemporary expression of the gospel. Indeed, interpretation of the gospel is precisely what Christians ought to be doing in response to the gospel. Yet the present proposal suggests that such interpretation (hermeneutics) will be faithful to the gospel if the outcome is a genuinely creative repetition of the gospel. What this amounts to is that there can be no such thing as simple or pure repetition. It is impossible. Creative repetition is required by the very character of God whose threefold repetition — of Father, Son, and Spirit — exemplifies the ideal of "freshness through sameness." Moreover, creative repetition is required by the concrete historical nature of human experience. Life goes on and demands new responses. The world is becoming increasingly complex; it is not the same as it was two thousand years ago. Good repetition is not achieved by simply imprinting what was said yesterday upon a new context; that is the way of domination. Accordingly, repetition is inescapable, and high-quality repetition emerges through attentiveness and discernment in the contingencies of life — that is, the context. Context is, after all, the weaving together of different textures.

Yet not all repetition of the gospel is successful. For example, the ideal of freshness through sameness is forfeited when the gospel is reduced to a "substancelike" quality. In this case the substance is equated with propositions of truth that are to be worded in precisely the same manner. Pure repetition is, on this view, a sign of faithfulness. Such repetition offers the illusion of security, but the price is high; the evangel is transposed into a form of doctrinal legalism. However, the real problems are transferred elsewhere — that is, into the practical sphere concerned with the application of the gospel. This procedure of establishing the right theory before attending to application gives the illusion of secure foundations, but such theology has forfeited freshness for a kind of sameness. Or perhaps the element of freshness is transferred to the question of application and practice of the truth. Is it any wonder that theology soon loses its vigor and appeal? It no longer witnesses to the freshness and creativity of God.

Another equally unsuccessful form of repetition occurs when the past is simply discarded. Creativity and freshness are sought, but this is thought to require severing links with the tradition. Often this amounts to newness for the sake of newness. This approach strikes a deep cord in Protestantism and produces an "occasionalism" of the Spirit; the Divine presence comes and goes; continuity is hard to discern. It seems that the idol of pure repetition has been firmly rejected; no sameness, only freshness. However, in this approach a new danger appears. In the quest for fresh spiritual vitality, a repetition reemerges under new guise; what is repeated is often nothing more than the profundities of human subjectivity. This is characterized by a fairly directionless, free-floating Christianity that becomes curved-in on the human subject and simply repeats a range of human thoughts uninformed by God's presence. The irony is inescapable; to end up communicating "just what I think" is to end up with sameness without freshness. In this climate the gospel suffers the worst fate; it becomes boring!

Our discussion points to the fact that we ought not be frightened of repetition but welcome it, seek to understand what we are doing, and allow our repeating of the good news to be informed by creative engagement with the gospel. Only in this way will evangelism be freed from systematically distorted communication. Such repetition will probably assume a variety of forms that facilitate "initiation into the Kingdom of God" (Abraham 1989).

With simplicity we have identified the basic complementarity between evangelism and theology, the former representing a concentrated expression of the latter's more extended discourse. This gave rise to repetition as a feature of both modes of communication. It should not go unnoticed that the challenge of repetition — of freshness through sameness — provides a useful theological heuristic through which to consider the importance of context in communication of the gospel. For example, when people refer to the importance of "contextual evangelism" (e.g., Costas) they are usually making a plea for a more creative and fresh repetition of the gospel that emerges out of the dynamic of a particular community's experience and praise of God. This can be contrasted to a *simple repetition* that fails to attend to the realities "on the ground" and to this extent imports into the communication unintended distortions. The result of this latter approach is that the evangel is no longer experienced as *good* news.

However, it might fairly be asked of the discussion so far, simplicity of what, repetition of what? Has not the discussion skirted around the main issue of the content of evangelism and theology? The issue of content has been implicit in what has already been said and has occasionally surfaced. It is time to treat this explicitly.

The Presence of Wisdom

It is possible to develop the notion of the content of the gospel in terms of the presence and nature of wisdom. This requires some further teasing out. Earlier it was suggested that evangelists and theologians were linked in the common task of communicating the praise of God. What is the content of such praise? Certainly, in Christian worship and discipleship praise is a dynamic activity focused on the gracious liberality of God concentrated in the life of Jesus and now present in the Spirit of the risen Christ. The notion of praise will be developed in the following chapters but for the moment we note that the term *praise* is used "to draw attention to the fundamental calling of the Christian disciple to glorify God, to live a life that recognizes and strives to make known the abundance of God's truth and justice in the world. Accordingly a life of praise is multifaceted, embracing the practical, emotional, moral, intellectual and religious elements of personal and social life" (UCA 1994:9). The content of such praise cannot be reduced to a set of propositions or truths for assent.

However, there is a form of doctrinalism in the church that quickly codifies the truth of the living God in such a way that the language of faith is set in certain fixed and tight forms. This is not to suggest that any language will do. But, unfortunately, the tendency to doctrinalize the truth *in this way* contributes to an image of God as lawgiver. In this context Christian beliefs are assented to as eternal laws. This approach to content often gives the impression that the good news is informationlike — a unique assemblage of facts. It suggests a theology of revelation that pays little heed to the rich modes of human experience within which the presence of God is manifest and fruitful. Christianity tends to be interpreted as an obediential religion within this information framework, though more often it is obedience without the joyfulness of the gospel. Under these conditions the purpose of evangelism is reduced to the communication of certain facts that will generate obedience to God: theology becomes a rather abstract rehearsal of the major and minor doctrines of particular Christian traditions.

It is true that we live in an information culture where power is vested in the holders and disseminators of information. Passing on knowledge is what it is all about, or so it might be construed. This is not to suggest that a form of "information apologetics" is unimportant in evangelism (Keck 1993:107). At a more popular level, the danger is that the gospel will quickly become a *product*. The real issue then becomes one of marketing to maximize "effectiveness" and "success." A systematically distorted gospel communication emerges, the praise of God is reduced to an information package, and wisdom quickly dissipates. Although the gospel may contain something of the character of information, it never can be *merely* information precisely because at its heart the gospel is the very presence of the living God in the midst of creation to transform and renew all things in the Spirit of Christ. Accordingly, to reduce the content of the gospel to information is a serious distortion of the form of Christian revelation.

What then may be an appropriate way in which to depict the content of the Christian community's praise of God? One possible answer, alluded to above, that has its roots deep within the Judeo-Christian tradition links our question about the content of praise to wisdom. The theme of wisdom has been an important influence in the shaping of

Christian identity. In the history of the interpretation of the gospel, the category of wisdom has made an important contribution. For example, Christian theology was, from early times, understood as a divine wisdom that brought illumination and salvation (Farley 1983). Such wisdom was never understood as a set of codified propositions nor simply the sum total of human thoughts. Rather, wisdom was a preeminently personal being, coming to concentration in Jesus and universalized through the Spirit of Christ (Hardy 1989:294ff). For the apostle Paul it was the wisdom of God in Christ crucified and risen that the Christian community witnessed to in the "evangel" (1 Cor. 1:18–2:8). This understanding of the gospel as the presence of God's wisdom has been an important focus for modern theology especially as it has drawn from insights of Christian feminism (Johnson 1993).

In the secular world, too, the theme of wisdom seems to be enjoying a renaissance in recent years (Sternberg 1990). But there is always a danger that overuse will lead to shallowness. It can easily become a synonym for well-honed common sense. In Christianity, however, wisdom is that which God bestows, and it is that to which all things are to be assimilated — that is, brought into relation with and changed accordingly (Hardy 1989:296f). Wisdom, as such, is the dynamic activity of God's presence lifting or raising created life to the fullness of truth, releasing ever more possibilities for life in the Spirit. This wisdom, born of the Spirit, is God's Christlike work in the world. Accordingly, it is this wisdom that is experienced and praised in the Christian community, repeated in its rich simplicity in evangelism, and meditated upon and unraveled in theological discourse.

Transformation: The Purpose of Communication

This chapter has offered a brief consideration of some of those dimensions of full and free speech relevant to evangelism and theology in the church. The essential structure of the relationship between evangelism and theology was developed through the theme of simplicity. The dynamic that generates a continued gospel communication was developed as an issue of repetition. The question of content was identified as the presence of wisdom. Simplicity as concentrated richness of truth, repetition as freshness through sameness, and wisdom as the form and content of God's presence are the three key norms that, under the constraint of the love of Christ (2 Cor. 5:14), guide the church's communication of the gospel.

However, a question arises as to what happens within such a communicative framework. In the Christian tradition the answer has been transformation through conversion. This occurs through communication in which an exchange takes place, an exchange not merely of information given and received but more fundamentally of the goodness of lives shared with God. When this is done well, human life is built up; it is raised to fuller heights with God and others. This points, however, to the fundamentally expansive nature of human life. It is capable of being added to quantitatively and qualitatively. This perfecting occurs through high-quality communication in which new and surprising possibilities for human life emerge and all participants in the activity undergo transformation. From this perspective, the Christian revelation provides a paradigm of communicative excellence witnessing throughout history to the transformative effects of the Divine presence in Christ and the Spirit. The nature of this gospel transformation is quite remarkable, for in it the past is transcended without being discounted or wasted; the old is taken up into something new (2 Cor. 5:17). In the resurrection, Jesus Christ did not leave his wounds behind (John 20:19–23). They belonged to his new life but in a new way. The end purpose of gospel communication is thus a transformed humanity within a transformed creation.

Accordingly, when we think of Christian conversion it might be helpful to consider it from the perspective of the potential of gospel communication to expand and build up human life in society. This begins through the bestowal of fresh understanding, energy, and direction, and this occurs as our lives are assimilated to God who is the wisdom, vitality, and sustainer of all creation. Certainly, this seemed to be the apostle Paul's experience on his missionary journeys throughout the Mediterranean. The gospel was shared, new communities were created where there were previously none, and human lives were reoriented, often in quite radical ways. A new and fresh wisdom for life had been generated from a Divine wisdom that had previously gone unrecognized (Acts 17:16–34). This higher wisdom was powerful enough to break the prevailing patterns of distorted wisdom and provide energy for fuller human communication that included a distinctive praise of a particular God (Grant 1986:19–83). This new reality was not abstract nor confined to individuals but primarily took root in the early communities of faith. These were often house churches where the God of the gospel was worshiped (Schillebeeckx 1988:40–73). It was this same God who, through the agency of the Spirit, gave an abundance of gifts for service in the world (Rom. 12:1–8; 1 Cor. 12:1–11; Eph. 4:11). The God of Jesus Christ was discovered to be sufficient for the affairs of this world, and it was this good news communicated with a simplicity and freshness over and over again in myriad contexts that constituted the life pulse of the early church.

Divine Agent: Gospel Communication

It has been suggested that evangelism and theology are complementary forms of human response to God's communication, that these modes of communication are guided by an appeal to simplicity, and that there is a bias toward repetition and the presence of wisdom. These three criteria provide conditions for faithful "wording" of the gospel that leads to human transformation. The linguistic domain of such communication is necessarily in view because the focus is quite specific — the relationship between two word-orientated forms of expression. However, a question arises as to why these three criteria. At one level, this chapter has offered an analysis of formal criteria (e.g., simplicity) operating in any vital communication, although even at this level the results have been valuable in highlighting the natural reciprocity between evangelism and theology. Yet throughout the discussion a deeper theological dynamic has been recognized — one that guides and shapes the way in which the formal criteria operate in Christian communication. At its heart this theological dynamic brings into focus the Divine agent at the center of the Christian story.

Who is this God? In the Christian tradition, God is praised as a being of communicative love. There is a simplicity to such a God — an abundance of richness in a highly concentrated form. This simplicity of God's being is repeated in self-differentiation — as Creator, Redeemer, and Fulfiller; Father, Son, and Spirit. In this repetition of God's simplicity, wisdom is discovered in the world and life is transformed. In the Scripture's narrative of salvation, the communion of God with the creation is concentrated in Jesus Christ and overflows in the presence of the Holy Spirit. This is the God who evokes human praise, who *informs* the communicative dynamic of the gospel. When this praise is repeated in evangelism and theology, the strength, love, and wisdom of God abounds. This gospel overflow of love manifests itself through a quality of communication that is open, free, respectful, and inviting. This communicative dynamic of the gospel is a fundamental ingredient in the liberation of the captives and the transformation of human society.

Conclusion

Our discussion points to the fact that the dynamics of gospel communication cannot be reduced to that of a human construct designed with purely pragmatic purposes in mind. Such a view easily avoids questions of accountability and responsibility. The inner coherence of the communication of the Christian faith requires, if it is to avoid problems associated with systematically distorted communication, a much richer understanding of the communicative process — one that makes space for the active presence of God in the communication. To allow this to occur in evangelism and theology seems to be precisely what is required for a genuinely critical theory of the gospel.

Recognition of the fundamental reality that God is the primary active agent in the gospel communication breeds both a confidence in such communication and an appropriate tone in such communication. It is a tone of respect and recognition for the One present in the communication from whom the endeavor to give voice to the gospel takes its cue.

It is also, by implication, a tone of respect and recognition for those with whom the evangel is shared. As the Christian community enters faithfully and joyfully into this activity through evangelism and theology, it offers true praise of God. This, at least, is the ideal, but it assumes a close link between evangelism and the Christian community. This assumption is examined in the following chapters. In doing so, we mark a transition from our inquiry into the relationship between evangelism and theology to the second major concern of this volume — the relationship between evangelism and the church. Chapters 4 and 5 thus take up the specifically ecclesiological issues that arise in evangelism.

4

A Community for the Praise of God

In Christ we were also chosen,... in order that we, who were
the first to hope in Christ, might be for the praise of his glory.
— Ephesians 1:11–12

A chapter entitled "A Community for the Praise of God"
might seem out of place in a discussion of evangelism.
However, the dynamics of communication outlined in the
foregoing chapter cannot stand alone without reference to
the life of the people of God. Although this may be granted
by many today, it is far from clear how a theology of evangelism derives its impulse from and in turn contributes in a
positive manner to the life of the church. The argument
of this chapter is that the communication of the gospel has an inescapable ecclesial form, that ecclesiology and
evangelism are inextricably linked, and that their complementary relationship is as important as that which obtains
between evangelism and theology. Through a discussion of
the relationship between evangelism and ecclesiology our
understanding of the dynamics of gospel communication
will be broadened and deepened.

At the outset we note a fundamental problem in the discussion and practice of evangelism as an activity of the

church. Specifically, it is not at all self-evident that evangelism is inescapably linked to the life of the Christian community. The question of *why* it is and *what* that might mean for the *form* of the church's evangelism is the subject of this chapter.

The Church of the Evangel

Within the modern period of evangelism the place of the church has been seriously neglected. The problem was recognized at the 1928 International Missionary Council in Jerusalem, where the "younger churches" argued that the indigenous "local church must be the center and point of departure for all missionary activity" (Gort 1978:282). Yet even the idea of a "church-centric" mission and evangelism often meant church and mission/evangelism as "two separate entities existing alongside each other" (:283). Within such a conception it was almost inevitable that one or other of these entities would dominate, the result being that church and evangelism might simply go their separate ways. Thus, despite the recognition of a problem, it is not surprising that ecclesiology has not been a major theme in evangelism in the modern period.

However, this problem is not peculiar to evangelism but is symptomatic of a more general loss of ecclesial consciousness that can be traced in the history of the Christian tradition, and not only within Protestantism. As a result, it is not clear that evangelism has an ecclesial form regardless of how much ink might be spilt recommending what the church should do to be an effective evangelizing church. I believe that this is a problem with George Hunter's popular and influential book on reaching secular people (1992). Why should "secular" people be "reached," for what purpose, and how might the church belong to this purpose? In other words, why join a church, even a relevant, modern, vibrant one envisaged by Hunter? Hunter seems to assume that being a people of the church does not require justification. In many respects, his book is not geared up to probe these kind of issues, for its primary concern is strategic. Insights are offered about the nature of "secular people" that can then become the basis for intelligent evangelistic planning. Some of the deeper theoretical issues about evangelism and church are not in view.

It is true that in more recent discussion the ecclesial dimension of evangelism has begun to emerge. It is a sign of health in Protestantism when theologies of evangelism include chapters on "Our Ecclesiology and Evangelism" (Larsen 1992) or "Church-Centered Evangelism" (Drummond 1992). However, the level of reintegration required here has not yet been achieved. The church is too often viewed simply as a tool for effective evangelism or the place to which evangelism will draw people. What a full-blown ecclesial consciousness with respect to evangelism might look like is not yet clear. Our best attempts so far have been somewhat piecemeal and testify to the difficulty of articulating the reality of the church within our conceptions of Christianity and its missional and evangelistic responsibilities. The most important efforts in this regard seem to come from those writers who have strong connections with the "base communities" of Latin America (Costas 1989). Thus Costas speaks of the church as "a fifth gospel," noting that "the gospel has been committed to a community, is transmitted by that community, and demands a community experience" (:134). He links the communitarian nature of evangelism to the "trinitarian community as evangelizing presence" (:71–87), though this promising start does not seem to be developed or play any significant part in his later discussion of the local congregation as "the base of evangelization" (:133ff).

William Abraham's logic of evangelism focuses on "initiation into the Kingdom of God" (1998), which he distinguishes from the concrete reality of the institutional church. This seems to be a deliberate attempt to give eschatology a higher profile in evangelism and allow for a critique of evangelistic approaches associated with the church-growth movement. Yet its strength is its weakness, for the actual relationship between the kingdom and the church remains blurred in his work, and, of more importance, his focus on "initiation" and "kingdom" precludes the development of a fuller ecclesial framework. It is not clear how or more particularly *why* the concrete reality of the church is important in the logic of evangelism. For example, is church simply the place where "initiation" occurs? How is God's reign related to being people of the church? If we are to be concerned with actual lived realities, then the concrete institutional life of the people of God has to be addressed more directly in evangelism particularly when, as with Abraham, the kingdom of God receives such strong focus. The danger of abstraction is ever present, and when it is all said and done, Abraham's notion of initiation looks very concrete and ecclesial after all. But whence comes this ecclesial form, and how is it related to the identity of God in the Christian tradition? Abraham's logic of evangelism appears to have a logical gap at this point, and my own sense is that this comes about because of his starting point with the kingdom. It may have some advantages over a more explicitly Trinitarian approach (Peters 1993:184ff), but Abraham has failed to show its significance for the *ecclesial nature* of Christianity.

The loss of ecclesial consciousness has been especially felt within Protestantism, where the place of the church has been somewhat marginal and rather too narrowly construed. There is a very good reason for this, as Friedrich Schleiermacher, the generally acknowledged father of modern Protestantism, noted in the early nineteenth century. In depicting the antithesis between Protestantism and Catholicism, he argued that "the former makes the individual's relation to the Church dependent on his relation to Christ, while the latter contrariwise makes the individual's relation to Christ dependent on his relation to the Church" (Schleiermacher 1960:103). This statement captures well a traditional fundamental difference in perception between these two major Christian communions. In Schleiermacher's view (ibid.) Protestantism, although holding fast to the reference to Christ, might forfeit "the Christian principle" by dissolving the communion; Roman Catholicism, although holding fast to this communion, was in danger of becoming unchristian "by neglecting the reference to Christ" (ibid.). Only the "spirit of Christianity" that prevailed in the church prevented these possibilities.

Much has happened since the early nineteenth century in missionary endeavors, ecumenics and theological insight across the ecclesial spectrum. The churches have learned from each other and continued to incorporate the best insights from others into their own self-understanding of mission and church. Indeed, within Protestantism the doctrine of the church has become a major locus for theological discussion. This was sharply put by the Lutheran theologian Jaroslav Pelikan when he suggested that the doctrine of the church had become "the bearer of the whole of the Christian message for the twentieth century, as well as the recapitulation of the entire doctrinal tradition from the preceding centuries" (1988:282). Pelikan, like many others, is pointing to the inescapable fact that Christianity is fundamentally a social phenomenon. The church cannot be tacked on at the end of a consideration of Christianity, nor ought it be regarded as the last event in a causal chain reaction, as it has tended to be treated in modern evangelism. *Church is nothing less than Christianity in its social form.* This is at the heart of Paul's affirmation: "You are the body of Christ, and each one of you is a part of it" (1 Cor. 12:27). The recovery of this insight is well summed up in the statement of the leading Roman Catholic scholar Karl Rahner: "A Christian has to be an ecclesial Christian" (1978:285).

This has been a hard pill for Protestants to swallow, and in some respects this difficulty can be well understood. A Protestant self-consciousness from the time of the Reformation has tended to view the development of the church as a social institution as evidence of a regression from a previously spontaneous Spirit-led communal life. In this scenario the institutionalization of Christianity's charismatic life eventually led to the extinction of the Spirit. This rather romanticized ideal of primitive Christian existence was, in part, a reaction to excessive claims made by Roman Catholicism for the institution of the church and the tendency this bred toward "sacralization" of the church and the consequent transformation of means into ends. This Protestant view was enshrined in Schleiermacher's comment noted above though it is clear that the Protestant response risked ignoring the church altogether. Yet the history of Protestantism has been one of ecclesial disputes and social fracturing on the pretext of holding faithfully to the "reference to Christ." Thus, although the ecclesial nature of Christianity disappeared theoretically, practically it consumed a great deal of energy and witnessed to significant disunity in the gospel, a situation that the modern missionary movement brought sharply into focus.

When Dietrich Bonhoeffer (1906–45) considered the matter in the early decades of this century, he saw the problem with a clarity that few had before or since. He developed a view of the church as "Christ existing as the community" (1963:160). The social form of Christianity was not a secondary matter but arose in (was given in) the relationship to God: "Communion with God exists only through Christ, but Christ is present only in His Church, hence there is communion with God only in the church. This fact destroys every individualistic conception of the Church" (:116).

It is precisely at this point that Bonhoeffer's insight is prophetic, for he identified a problem at the heart of modern Christianity, that is, its radically individualist nature. These days we are quite familiar with our Enlightenment inheritance as regards the philosophy of the individual. Certainly, we are familiar with the impact of this for church life and evangelism in recent times. The problem of excessively individualistic and privatized notions of Christianity is inescapable. It constitutes what the Lutheran theologian Edward Farley calls the "contemporary peril" of the church: "Individualism, the contemporary form of the Church's repression of its ecclesial dimension, is so close to us, so very much a part of us that it is almost beyond thematization" (1975:182). The force of individualism can be discerned across a range of theological and church traditions and becomes evident in "the omission of ecclesia in the formulation of the situation of faith and the pursuit of theological themes" (ibid.). Farley argues that a high focus on the institutionality of Christianity per se can simply mask the fact that "face-to-face relation is displaced by the anonymity of the large and economically successful congregation" (:185). These words, written two decades ago, have a somewhat prophetic ring about them in view of the emergence of the phenomenon of the megachurches of the West.

However, the problem of individualism and the modern church is complex, and there are no quick-fix solutions. It has taken many generations to develop, and the lure of cheap detours around the problem must be resisted. In the first instance we need to recognize the extent and complexity of the problem. The spirit of "anti-institutionalism" of modern society generates both a lack of confidence in and even disdain for institutional life, including church life, and, ironically, an increasing drive to forms of social life that idolize institutions. This latter development is evidenced in the church in forms of exclusivism in which "individual piety and religious experiences replace collective memory" and "provincial space and concern for fellowship replaces the space perpetually drawing in the stranger" (ibid.). The secular version of this has been identified by Robert Bellah as "lifestyle enclaves" (1986:72). Thus, in an increasingly fragmented culture, the alienated individual's drive for security overreaches itself. This occurs most obviously by rejection of all authority structures. However, it can also occur by a retreat into rigid and enclosed social structures. In this latter phenomenon, private personal security is fostered in direct proportion to the capacity of the institution to enforce uniformity and suppress individual differences. It leads to an affirmation of group identity along the lines of "We're OK; we're all individuals but we all believe and act the same here." Institutional tyranny masks the insecurities of alienated individualism; the quest for societal cooperation and justice involves denial of individual differences (Hauerwas 1981:83).

What is lacking in the above is any genuine experience of community in which face-to-face relations provide a norm for human existence both within and beyond particular social groups. In fact, the individualist ethic of modernity generates what might be termed an *acommunal bias* in social life — not so much a conscious rejection of communal life but an inbuilt predisposition in which interpersonal orientations are already skewed toward the autonomous, independent, and competitive individual (UCA 1994:14fn3). It is in the light of this peril that the church of Jesus Christ is called to realize in word and deed the good news of the gospel — to be a bearer of this good news for the world. In other words, within the context of late modernity the evangel will have to be lived and witnessed to in such a manner that *new community* becomes a real possibility, where the captives to the individualist philosophy of the times are freed for life together. This can no longer be an optional extra, nor ought it be viewed as something secondary to the nature of the gospel itself. This would be to perpetuate the false notion that Christianity is primarily a private, individual matter.

On the basis of the above, it is clear that evangelism, if it is intended to be good news for the peoples of the world, will have to be news of a God who brings to birth new communities where the joys, difficulties, disappointments, and responsibilities of human life in this world are woven together with the Spirit of peace. What is thus "good" about such a gospel is not only that it is personal but that it is *simultaneously communal.* Given the condition of modernity identified above, the evangel could not be experienced as "good" if it is not both together. From this perspective, to include the question of the church in a discussion of evangelism does not signal a retreat into a cloistered, inward-looking Christianity but rather indicates a serious attempt to pinpoint the resonance of the gospel within contemporary Western cultures. Out of faithfulness to the gospel, *in this context evangelism will have to be fundamentally ecclesial in orientation and character*. Similarly, the character and orientation of the church will have to be directed unambiguously and wholeheartedly by the glad tidings of God for the world, or, as Wilbert Shenk states, the church will have to be reconceptualized in terms of "the Great Commission" (:108).

However, to recognize the ecclesial nature of Christianity as intrinsic to the gospel is not simply a good strategic move within the culture of late or postmodernity. There is a deeper *theological* reason both as to why the church is intrinsic to the evangelistic dynamic of the gospel and why it has proved to be exceedingly difficult to give full play to this requirement. Perhaps not surprisingly, this reason has to do with the identity of the God of the gospel. To this subject we now briefly turn.

The God of the Gospel

Who is the God to whom the Christian community offers praise through worship and discipleship in the world? The identity of this God is narrated in the Scriptures as the God of Abraham, Isaac, Sarah, and Ruth, of Jesus the Messiah and the church that bears the name of Christ. This is the pilgrim God who is always moving out, searching for, visiting, gathering together, and building up the pilgrim people; the God who does not remain "aloof" but travels to the "far country" to seek and save (Barth 1956b:158). This is the God who both sends and is sent (cf. John 14 and 15). In the

Christian tradition the character of this "apostolic" form of God's activity has been succinctly stated in the following:

> Apostolicity denotes an outward-directed movement of God. The classical doctrine of the *missio dei,* the mission of God, speaks of God's apostolic nature. It depicts God's own pilgrimage in the creation and redemption of the world through Jesus and the Spirit. The trinitarian pattern of this movement commended itself to the early church in the light of its inherited Jewish monotheism and its experience of new life in the Spirit of the crucified and resurrected Jesus Christ. This apostolic dynamic of the triune God is illustrated richly in biblical imagery: in the God who, as a shepherd, actively moves out to seek the lost; who, with an authoritative word, confronts Pharaoh and liberates the captives; who, like a loving parent, waits with impatient longing to welcome the wayward offspring home (UCA 1994:10).

This apostolic dynamic was identified in Chapter 3 in terms of the simplicity, repetition, and wisdom of the God of the gospel. It is this God who, through Christ, reconstitutes human community wherein the Spirit dwells. For example, in the letter to the fledgling church at Ephesus the writer refers to Christ as the peacemaker, the one who "has made the two one and has destroyed the barrier, the dividing wall of hostility" (Eph. 2:14). Henceforth, through the cross Christ has reconciled Jew and Gentile such that "both have access to the Father by one Spirit" (2:18), and Gentiles are now "fellow citizens with God's people and members of God's household" (2:19). Here, in embryo, is the basis for the new community of God's people. People who "once were far away" (2:13) have been brought near to God, old barriers have been demolished, enmity has been set aside. In such a new community differences are not negated nor do they continue to exert abusive power and determine relationships. Rather, conditions have been established for a community of peace and hospitality through the Spirit of God. The way of peace was the way of nondomination. However, as the New Testament shows, this ideal had to be worked at and struggled for through the many conflicts that beset the early Christian church and its missionary endeavors. To be a community with a passion for the gospel, open and inviting to the wider society; indeed eager to go out as bearers of the glad tidings of God, constituted the apostolic brief of the Christian church. The emerging church was a "sent people," witnesses to the God of Jesus Christ.

Implicit in the above is a communitarian understanding of the being of God. The Christian tradition has given voice to this Divine character as the triune God. The God of the gospel creates new human community because *sociality belongs to the very identity of the God praised in the Christian church* (Gunton 1993:219–23). The nature of this Divine community that comes to its fullness in Jesus Christ and continues in the Spirit has been a controversial and persistent preoccupation in the Christian tradition. Indeed, the fortunes of this discussion provide the deep background to much of our present difficulties in relating church and evangelism. What justification is there for this statement? Here we do well to recall that the Western tradition has had great difficulty in maintaining a clear and committed hold to a doctrine of the Trinity that takes seriously the concreteness of God's being as depicted in the classical form as Father, Son, and Holy Spirit. The tendency in the Western tradition has been to collapse the distinctions into an overarching unity. Thus, in theology the doctrine of God (e.g.,

Aquinas) was developed first in relation to the unity of God and only then were the Trinitarian distinctions derived. In this context the Triune character of God was always in danger of collapsing into an undifferentiated monotheism. This theoretical problem was manifest at the practical level of Christian piety, as Karl Rahner observed some years ago: "Despite their orthodox confession of the Trinity, Christians are, in their practical life, almost mere 'monotheists.' We must be willing to admit that, should the doctrine of the Trinity have to be dropped as false, the major part of religious literature could well remain virtually unchanged" (1970:10).

As a result, the West has struggled to retain its Trinitarian consciousness. This has been well documented in more recent theology in the writings of, for example, Jürgen Moltmann (1981). From this perspective it is perhaps unsurprising that the doctrine of the church has not, until recent times at least, been particularly well developed, the reason being that a loss of Trinitarian consciousness goes hand in hand with a loss of ecclesial consciousness. Similarly, the recovery of the genuinely communitarian character of the God of the gospel, with its basis in Jesus' self-differentiation from God the Father and the Spirit (Pannenberg 1991:308–19), has provided a critical impetus to the emergence of a renewed interest in the church as the community called to live for the praise of God's name, an echo as it were of the Divine community (Gunton and Hardy 1989:69). *In short the evangel is community forming precisely because the God of the Christian gospel is a being of loving and hence overflowing communion.* For this reason the identity of God narrated in the Scriptures, worshiped in the church, and served in the world provides the ultimate horizon for any attempt to articulate the logic of evangelism in contemporary theology. When sight is lost of this horizon, conditions emerge for systematically distorted communication of the good news: the transformative power of God is unable to provide the resource for the evangelism impulse in the church. Moreover, it is only as space is given for this God to come into view that it becomes abundantly clear that the church can no longer be ignored or simply forgotten in the evangelism equation; that evangelism, if it is to be faithful to the gospel, must arise from within the life of the church. Furthermore, it is precisely because of the link between the gospel and the church that a theology of evangelism will have to take its cue from a fuller understanding of the nature and calling of the people of God to be a community of praise.

A Community of Praise

If the God of the gospel provides the *ultimate* horizon for a theology of evangelism then, it is equally true to refer to the church as constituting the *intermediate* horizon for evangelism. The two horizons are related insofar as the *source* of our understanding of the church is the doctrine of the Trinity, an affirmation increasingly prevalent in the literature on evangelism (e.g., Costas). However, a question remains as to how such a God is related to the visible historical community of faith or, from our present perspective, how the Christian community offers concrete witness to its faith in God. In other words, what is the ecclesial dynamic appropriate to the way in which God works in the world — a dynamic that corresponds to and complements the communicative dynamic of the gospel discussed in Chapter 3?

One way of approaching this set of questions is to begin

by asking about the purpose of the church. There are admittedly many different ways of expressing purpose, though it is not simply the case that one is as good as another. At this point we follow the logic of our discussion above concerning the character of the God of the gospel. Here we pointed to the "apostolic" character of the pilgrim God. A corollary of this is that the people of God are called to be apostolic; their fundamental purpose is encapsulated in the notion of being "sent people." This identity and purpose makes a church an evangelizing church: "Certainly a Church which is not as such an evangelizing Church is either not yet or no longer the Church, or only a dead Church, itself standing in supreme need of renewal by evangelization" (Barth 1962:874). The good news is intrinsically overflowing news as the first letter of Peter describes it: "You are a chosen people, a royal priesthood, a holy nation, a people belonging to God, that you may declare the praises of him who called you out of darkness into his wonderful light" (2:9). This might be thought of as constituting the Petrine form of the "great commission" of Matthew's Gospel (chap. 28). This depiction of the identity, calling, and hence purpose of the church would no doubt resonate with many today.

However, it is tempting to move too quickly into strategic planning for evangelism; to organize the "declaring" of the gospel. What might be easily forgotten is that what is to be declared is "the praise of God." Declaring the praise of God cannot be reduced simply to delivering the message, a sort of information package as referred to in the previous chapter, no matter how modern and appealing it may appear. This is a trap I believe George Hunter's manifesto for reaching secular people succumbs to when, in his discussion of "the theology we communicate," he places significant emphasis on "doctrines" and "truth claims," and "a functionally reduced canon," albeit in the name of revivifying the Christian message (1992:91–97). Rather, to "declare the praise of God" generates an expectation that we are to go and tell the gospel in a manner that honors the One to whom our ultimate praise is offered. In other words, the people of God are called to bear witness to the gospel in a praiseworthy manner. This, of course, is the rub in much evangelism that often fails to evidence true praise of God or, contrary to its best intentions, organizes true praise out of the picture altogether!

Form and content cannot be torn apart. When this has happened, the consequences have been disastrous in the history of Christian missions. If the message is one that evokes right praise of God, then the manner of the communication ought to embody the praiseworthiness of that same God. Barth saw the issue clearly: "What is vital is that the evangelizing community should say what it has to say to those around *in a glad and spirited and peaceful way corresponding to its content*" (1962:874; my italics). In terms of Habermas's analysis, the "acts of communication" (i.e., evangelistic practices) ought to embody and serve "communicative action" in which the orientation is toward mutual understanding. Yet for the Christian community, full mutual understanding cannot be achieved without a fundamental reference to the God of the gospel, a reference that, if it is genuine, will manifest itself in the form and ethos of the communication. Accordingly, Christians are those called to go and tell the glad tidings with *gladness.* This requires some further expansion, but the base line here is that praise is the human reflex to the outflow of God's love in Jesus Christ. This seems to resonate with the hope expressed in the letter to the Ephesians wherein we read that "we, who were the first to hope in Christ, might be for the praise of his glory" (1:1). Certainly, a life of praise is precisely what is envisaged for the saints of heaven, according to the writer of Revelation: "Then a voice came from the throne, saying, 'Praise our God, all you his servants, you who fear [God], both great and small!'" (19:5).

It is this element of praise that is picked up by the missionary, bishop, and theologian Lesslie Newbigin when he states that the first characteristic of the community of Jesus Christ will be praise. "It will be a community of praise. That is perhaps its most distinctive character" (1989:227). Newbigin goes on to note that praise "is an activity which is almost totally absent from 'modern' society" (ibid.), an absence, notes Barth, that constitutes "a yawning gulf in the life of the world" (1962:865). However, to speak of praise can lead to misunderstanding, for the word is often associated with particular forms of worship and church life. In this present discussion praise is intended in its broadest possible sense, reminiscent of the historic expression of the first statement of the *Shorter Catechism* of 1647: "Man's [sic] chief end is to glorify God and enjoy him forever" (Schaff 1990:676). Thus, recalling our discussion in Chapter 3, the term "praise" draws attention to the calling of the Christian disciple to "glorify God." Such a life of praise "is multifaceted, embracing the practical, emotional, moral, intellectual and religious elements of personal and social life" (UCA 1994:9; cf. Keck 1993:27–33). Insofar as this praise takes place in the world. it points to the fact that praise is an outward-directed activity enriching all life. For this reason praise is "inherently missional in character, seeking to respond to God's own praise of life poured out in creation and redemption through Jesus Christ and the Spirit" (UCA:10).

The above argument leads to a notion of the church as a community that exists for the praise of God. This approach is not particularly new, being rooted in our Christian tradition in Scripture, liturgy, poetry, and theology. In the Psalms praise is a response recognizing that "God has triumphed" (Brueggemann 1993:14). Indeed, the theme of praise is the "over-arching theme of the book of Psalms" (Keck 1993:29), though eventually, as in Psalm 150, even the psalmist offers praise for no particular reason (ibid.). Stephen Sykes, in "An Anglican Theology of Evangelism," identifies the significance of praise in worship (1991). He finds echoes of this theme in the early seventeenth-century poetry of George Herbert, whose poem "Gratefulness" captures well the piety of Herbert's inherited liturgical tradition.

> Thou that hast giv'n so much to me,
> Give one thing more, a grateful heart . . .
> Not thankful, when it pleaseth me;
> As if thy blessings had spare days:
> But such a heart, whose pulse may be Thy praise.

This same rich note is struck in the contemporary poetry, prayers, and hymns of the American writer Thomas Troeger (1994). In recent years the centrality and power of praise for the shaping of the Christian theological tradition has been recognized in a sustained piece of systematic theology (Hardy and Ford, 1984; cf. Wainwright 1980). Praise is indeed an essential of Christian community; it is that "which constitutes the community and its assemblies," and for this reason it is the first and "special ministry" of the Christian community (Barth 1962:866). Barth is worth quoting at length here: "To praise God, as a function in the ministry of the Christian community, is to affirm, acknowledge, approve, extol and laud both the being of God as the One who in His [sic] eternal majesty has become man, and the action in which He has taken man, all men, to Himself in His omnipotent mercy. It is to magnify the God who in this being and action of His is our God, Emmanuel, with us and for us. It is to confess Him publicly as the only true God" (:865). Although such praise has myriad forms, Barth's Reformed focus is on speech. However, his conclusion, perhaps somewhat surprising but no less welcome, would surely resonate across the ecclesial spectrum: "Singing is the highest form of human expression . . . [such that] the community which does not sing is not the community" (:867). Accordingly, the "praise of God which finds its concrete culmination in the singing of the community is one of the indispensable basic forms of the ministry of the community" (ibid.). This proposal has received ample confirmation in the contemporary renewal of song and music (and dance!) in the Christian church, from the charismatic Pentecostal wing to the more liturgically orientated communities such as Taizé and Iona. This renewal in song has proved to be a critical factor in the evangelistic impulse of the church, not least because the authentic sound of the gospel, when sung and celebrated attracts, convicts, and transforms those who hear its echo.

Our discussion of the theme of praise points to the fact that it is not simply another element alongside other activities and purposes for the church of Jesus Christ. Rather, "Christians know, if not by instinct then certainly through their spiritual formation, that praise lies at the heart of their identity" (Donnelly 1992:39). In the words of the contemporary German poet Rainer Maria Rilke, "to praise is the whole thing" (ibid.). It is the fundamental dynamic that gives energy and direction to that community led by the Spirit of the God of Jesus. Accordingly, whatever the church does, whatever activities and responsibilities it assumes, whatever service it offers in the name of Christ, whatever causes it pursues in the name of justice and truth ought ideally occur within an environment suffused with the praise of God. Precisely because of its importance, Barth's warning needs to be heeded: "Praise is the most endangered and dangerous undertaking in the church" (1968:124). A certain vigilance is necessary lest praise be forgotten or distorted and unfaithful to the God of the gospel. Yet as the church enters into the spirit of praise, it offers testimony to the presence and action in the world of the Holy Spirit. It was John Calvin who spoke of the Divine Spirit, even before the beauty of the world was displayed, "cherishing the confused mass," "being diffused over all space, sustaining, invigorating, and quickening all things ... transfusing vigor into all things, breathing into them being, life, and motion" (Calvin, *Institutes:* Bk. 1, chap. 13, par. 14). This same sense of the presence and action of God is the reason for the exhortation in Psalm 150: "Let everything that has breath praise the Lord."

On this account praise of God is clearly relevant to Christian worship (Keck 1993:23–42), but it cannot be simply restricted to this form of ecclesial life. As Walter Brueggemann points out, there is a dynamic in Israel's praise that has its source in liturgy and an impulse that is inherently missional: " 'Telling among the nations' about the new governance, which is what Israel does in praise, has extraordinary social and missional significance.... That mission of 'telling among the nations' (which is not Western, not imperialistic, not committed to an economic ideology) depends on faithful liturgy. Missional testimony to the nations cannot take place until a new world of social possibility and theological governance is imagined, and that imagining is primarily liturgical" (1988:158f). For Israel, praising worship involved a reconfiguring of the world; the outcome of such praise "is another world marked by justice, mercy, and peace" (:160). The implication is clear for the Christian church: true praise will necessarily reach into the myriad ways in which disciples of Christ follow the leading of the pilgrim God in the world. A community for the praise of God is a multifaceted and richly variegated community, the sheer variety testifying to the infinite possibilities and contexts that exist for expressing praise. This is one of the reasons why a good deal of contemporary literature on evangelism, including official church and ecumenical documents (Scherer and Bevans 1992), has ranged over a whole range of areas to do with worship (Armstrong 1986; Drane 1994), ministerial leadership (Armstrong 1984), pastoral care and spiritual guidance (Johnson 1991), preaching (Larsen 1992), lifestyle (Aldrich 1988), service (Armstrong 1979), ethics and morals (Haring 1991), rural contexts (Ruffcorn 1994), cities (Greenway and Monsma 1989), and social action (Boff 1991; Costas 1989). A common thread through much of this material is a focus on the local congregation (Green; 1990 Marshall 1990) and initiation into the kingdom (Abraham 1989). It points to the fact that the announcement of the glad tidings of the gospel cannot be too narrowly construed or be disconnected from the rest of Christian life and discipleship in the world.

Conclusion

The above proposal is not simply that praise is the *context* or *environment* for church and thus evangelism. That would be only partially true and could lead to the view that evan-

gelism might be one way in which the church offered praise
to God. Although this is quite true, something more is intended. Praise of God is not only the object of the church's
life and activities; praise is the impulse that energizes and
directs the Christian community in its communicative life.
The One whom the people of God praise, the activities
through which this is embodied, and the way or ethos with
which such activities are engaged in are intimately related.
Praise informs the content, form, and dynamic for the life
of the church. Thus the evangelism ethic, the integrity
of its strategic actions, are to be measured not simply by
faithfulness to the gospel understood in terms of information correctness but by the conformity of its practices to
God's own way of bestowing grace and praise upon creation
through Jesus and the Spirit. In other words, if the church's
evangelism is to be truly liberating, it will have to follow
the way of praise *in all its parts.* What this might involve is
explored in our concluding Chapter 5.

5

Liberating the Captives:
A Praise-Centered Evangelism

―――――

It is for freedom that Christ has set us free.
— Galatians 5:1a

"Mozart does not *will* to proclaim the praise of God. He just does it — precisely in that humility in which he himself is, so to speak, only the instrument with which he allows us to hear what he hears: what surges at him from God's creation, what rises in him, and must proceed from him" (Barth 1956c:37f). Barth's appreciation of Mozart is well known. He began each morning listening to Mozart, he died with the sound of Mozart in his ear, and no doubt very soon after would have heard him again in heaven before meeting Augustine, St. Thomas, Luther, Calvin, and Schleiermacher (:16). The secret of Mozart's praise of God was quite simple: he did not will it; it simply arose within him and overflowed as he listened. Evidently, praise of God is not something that can be manufactured, willed, or controlled. What then is the dynamic by which true praise arises and overflows, and how might this be relevant to our understanding of evangelism? The question is clearly important within the overall discussion of this book, particularly in the light of the definition of evangelism proposed by Hardy and Ford: "The content of praise repeated and explained to others so that they may join the community of Jesus Christ" (:19; cf. the fuller discussion 149–52). Accordingly, this final chapter inquires into the nature of that praise through which freedom can flourish.

Evangelism: The "Horizontal" Dimension of Praise

Evangelism has been referred to as the "horizontal dimension" of our praise of God in contradistinction to the "vertical dimension" of worship and prayer (ibid.). This distinction between vertical and horizontal dimensions of praise is useful, not least because it calls attention to what we have already observed above, namely, that praise occurs in the life of the Christian community in many ways of which evangelism is one. In this case it is an activity in which the goodness of God is shared with others. As such it is a communicative activity that includes a range of mediums for its expression but nevertheless is particularly focused on communication through language. This focus is suggested in the activity of "repeating and explaining" the gospel. Sharp delineation of modes of expression at this point is unnecessary and is in fact quickly overturned by the actual ways in which evangelism works. Moreover, the attempt to restrict or widen the ambit of what constitutes evangelism (e.g., proclamation and/or social action) usually ends in a rather sterile argument that only betrays the prejudices of its proponents. In any case, the drift of the present discussion is in another direction as we explore the primary theological dynamics at work in the church's evangelism. In particular, this final chapter examines further the proposal by Hardy and Ford that "praise is the primary form of the communication of the gospel, the sheer enjoyment and appreciation of it before God, 'even when there is no point at all'" (:149). With this in mind I argue in this chapter for an evangelism that is praise centered.

However, in order to pursue the notion of a praise-centered evangelism, it is necessary to develop in greater detail the way Christian praise of God operates and its relationship to the evangelistic calling of the church. At this point we follow the clues offered by Hardy and Ford in identifying two essential elements in the dynamics of praise — what may be termed *penitential praise* and *celebratory praise*. The former is a response of praise out of thankfulness for forgiveness. The latter, although not unrelated to the former, is fundamentally a joyful response to the God of all joy (Rom. 15:13).

Elements of Praise: Evangelism's Penitential Aspect

When individuals and communities confess their sins to God, they explicitly acknowledge the One who is the ultimate source of forgiveness. The context for this activity is usually worship, whether corporately or in the life of personal devotion. However, the act of recognition and acknowledgment that it is the God of Jesus Christ in whom forgiveness, acceptance, and restoration is secured is a primary form of human praise of God. By going to this God and not other gods, Christians witness to the fact that this is the living God who alone is worthy of honor and heartfelt thanks for lives renewed. From this perspective it is thus appropriate to speak of a praise that is penitential in form. In the Christian tradition, the *Confessions* of St. Augustine provide one of the most sustained acts of praise to the

God who forgives, restores, and renews (Hardy and Ford 1984:15f, 139). Augustine quite deliberately places his exposition of the heart of a penitent within the framework of his desire to offer true praise to God. Thus, in the opening paragraph Augustine asks: "Can any praise be worthy of the Lord's majesty?...Man [sic] is one of your creatures, Lord, and his instinct is to praise you....He is part of your creation, he wishes to praise you. The thought of you stirs him so deeply that he cannot be content unless he praises you, because you made us for yourself and our hearts find no peace until they rest in you" (Augustine 1961 translation:21). The *Confessions* link up with the whole biblical tradition of penitential praise evidenced perhaps most profoundly and poignantly in the Psalms, the sinner's prayer book. Here the whole breadth of human failure and evil is brought before God. Even the prayers themselves often testify to the subtle entrapment of sin in human life: it seems that the psalmist would have God destroy those who have brought harm (e.g., Psalm 137). Nothing it seems is held back from the Lord. The corollary is clear: there is nothing that cannot be forgiven, everything can become the occasion for a recovery of right praise.

This was the tradition in which St. Paul, one-time persecutor of the people of the Way, stood when he testified that nothing could separate God's people from the love of God in Christ Jesus (Rom. 8:31–39). It was the gospel tradition exemplified in Peter's denial of Christ and eventual restoration; of Mary who anointed Jesus with expensive oil as sign of a forgiven and thankful life; of the thief on the cross whose turning to Christ was greeted with acceptance and blessing; and of Thomas, whose unbelief was transformed into the confession "My Lord and my God." In this common tradition of penitential praise, God is honored as the One who forgives and awakens human life out of what Barth calls "slothful" sin (Barth 1958:403). As human beings are enabled through grace to respond to God in this way, they discover new resources from Christ, the life-giving Spirit (1 Cor. 15:45). For Christians are those who, in Barth's metaphor, are continually "awakened" by God for service in the kingdom (:553ff).

Evangelism is closely related to penitential praise. Indeed, the Western tradition has been particularly strong in its emphasis on the perilous condition of the guilty human being in consequence of the sin that clings so tightly, of the need for a radical turning to God, of the need for grace if restoration is to be effected. Yet, as Calvin long ago recognized, this orientation can easily be skewed in the wrong direction (Calvin, *Institutes:* Bk. 3, chap. 3, par. 4ff). In this case "evangelical repentance," signifying the appropriate response to God's love and mercy in Christ — the sinner "looks up and sees in Christ the cure of his wound" — is displaced by "legal repentance," the latter "a kind of threshold to hell" representing that repentance which leaves the sinner overwhelmed by sin and God's judgment but "unable to escape from it." Although Calvin argued that forgiveness could not be obtained *without* repentance, legal repentance operated on the wholly false assumption that repentance was the *cause* of forgiveness and failed to account for the giftlike character of repentance (Bk. 3. chap. 3, par. 21; chap. 4, par. 3).

Such was Calvin's complaint about the medieval penitential system. Yet in the history of Western Christianity this legal repentance has dominated and fed into what has aptly been referred to as the "introspective conscience of the West" (Stendahl 1973). One of the victims of this unhealthy religious dynamic has been the gospel itself! When conditional forgiveness hangs like a cloud over human life, the consequences are, as Karl Barth so clearly indicated, disastrous: God's NO appears more significant than God's YES. Not only does the efficaciousness of God's grace seem at the mercy of human freedom; the latter becomes entrapped in a downward spiral of self-loathing and despair for the very good reason that no amount of repentance can earn divine forgiveness. The point is that the gospel does not work like that, though to be sure the natural human intuition about such matters would seem to and is evidenced in some approaches to evangelism. However, in such contexts the gospel is no longer experienced as good news. The captives remain captives despite all rhetoric to the contrary. In terms of our earlier discussion, the preaching of a conditional forgiveness as outlined above represents the intrusion of systematically distorted communication. A mistaken or rather unexamined assumption about the fundamental character of the church's gospel generates distorted strategic actions, one result being that the gospel cannot be received as good news!

Yet the religious impulse is so powerful and the desire for liberation is so great that human beings either seek it elsewhere (Roberts 1996:189–95) or, as Christians, live half-lives, willing for God to forgive what appears mildly pardonable but resistant to a full opening of the human heart for fear that such disclosure can be neither accepted by God nor borne by the repressed self. What thus emerges is a truncated form of humanity that never realizes what it means to "learn to be a sinner" (Hauerwas 1983:30f), unable to be a true and full penitent and consequently never able to enter into the life of praise that comes from the unconditional forgiveness of the gospel. Evangelical repentance generates penitential praise. This is good news, for in

it the captives can find freedom and joy. It is precisely what
the West needs to recover in the dynamic of contemporary
evangelism. This is particularly the case in the critical area
of evangelistic preaching, for here it is very easy to slide
into a conditional grace that says, in effect: "'If you do
this...then God will do....' This is a very different gospel from the one announced by the preacher in the form,
'Because God has done this...therefore you can....'" (for
discussion of this important issue see Niedenthal 1980).

Elements of Praise: Evangelism's Celebratory Aspect

The liberation that comes through penitential praise has the
potential to blossom into true celebratory praise. This celebratory note belongs to the music of the gospel and points
to the fact that at its heart evangelism represents an overflow of appreciation and delight in the God of all joy. Such
overflow cannot be held back but rather seeks release and
communication to others. This seems to be part of the inner
logic of the Christian gospel. It points to the fact that as
we enter into the praise of God others are captivated and
drawn in; a longing for others to share in our delight inten-
sifies. From this perspective it is right to speak of a spiral
of praise that emerges through our faltering, stammering,
and often impure praise of God. In this spiral an echo of
true praise of God can be heard. The Song of Songs is
an unlikely text in this regard. However, the mutual delight of the two lovers and their respectful but generous
responses to each other reveal something of the dynamic
of praise. The lover and the beloved bestow honor upon
each other, male power is relinquished, and delight through
intimacy arises (Trible 1978:160). Moreover, the encounter
points to the fundamentally expansive character of praise

wherein the lover's delight in the other overflows: "Awake, north wind, and come, south wind! Blow on my garden, that its fragrance may spread abroad" (4:16a). Such delight cannot remain locked up; it has a dynamic of its own that cannot but expand, a release of praise for the sake of the beauty that has been found.

This was familiar to the Paul of Ephesians, who spoke of the "fragrance" of Christ's self-offering to God (Eph. 5:2) and sought to be an imitator of Christ (1 Cor. 11:1) — knowing Christ and the power of his resurrection, sharing in the fellowship of his sufferings, "becoming like him in his death" in the hope of resurrection from the dead (Phil. 3:10). Such an imitation of God (Eph. 5:1) gave a momentum and fragrance to Paul's life that took him all over the Mediterranean world for the sake of the One who had become his praise and delight. Even more remarkable for Paul was the discovery that in each place where the gospel was announced the presence of Christ became manifest and lives were changed. "The astonishing missionary journeys of St. Paul seemed to be motivated, not simply as the result of a personal call, sustained by the companionship of Christ. They had more to do with his discovery of the presence of the risen Christ in the world itself. He found that the world was not empty but filled with the presence of Christ — a Christ-like place, so much so that traveling the world was for him a constant finding of Christ. And he found that the peoples of the world were themselves Christ-like; speaking to them was a constant rediscovering of Christ" (Hardy 1989:46). Such a view of mission provides a much broader and richer framework for the church's announcement of the evangel to the world. Its basis is not in the absence of God but rather the superabundance of God's presence in Jesus Christ in the world, an abundance that inspired confidence and a celebratory praise. But for Paul and the early church, this way of praise was not an occasion for a triumphalism. Indeed, many of the early conflicts indicated just how important it was that the Christian praise of God should not degenerate into a self-aggrandizement but rather retain the servant way of Jesus (Phil. 2:1–12), a way that was, for Paul, a natural response to the superabundance of grace in Jesus Christ (1 Tim. 1:14).

This foundation of praise of God out of the plenitude of God constituted the heart of the gospel preached by Jesus in his parables (the pearl of great price, Matt. 13:46), enacted in his ministry (feeding of the 5000, Matt. 14:13–21), and captured in Jesus' words: "I have come that they may have life, and have it to the full" (John 10:10). In other words the gospel of Jesus was, from the earliest times, a dynamic overflow of new life derived from a life in which everything was referred to God. Such was the movement of praise (Hardy and Ford 1984:126). For the apostle Paul, this surprising and extravagant "how much more" of the gospel (Rom. 5:15–21) represented "the 'odd' *logic of superabundance*" wherein an "ordinary 'logic' collapses and the 'logic' of God ... blows up" (Ricoeur 1975:138). As people and communities responded to this surprising, energizing freshness of life, they too became participants in the abundance of God's love; they found themselves in the "slipstream" of a reality that they, like Mozart, simply had to give voice to. This dynamic provides a distinctly *theological* rationale for the spread of Christianity that was rapid on any account — a fact recognized by even the more dispassionate of classical historians: "Christians spread and increased: no other cult in the Empire grew at anything like the same speed" (Fox 1986:271). We should also note that the forms in which this gospel was expressed were many and varied; for example, hospitality, apologetic and intellectual debate, martyrdom, and so forth. We should also note that traditional categories in evangelism such as "witness" take on new meaning from the perspective of praise. No longer does witness denote a dry, obediential, or heroic religion but rather a dynamic and joyful activity borne of a "humble happiness" or "liberating certainty" of life with Jesus Christ (Jossua 1985:49). Such witness, which "comes about in a community and has its roots there" (:43), truly liberates and makes possible "the dawning of God in a human life" (:88).

Praising God: Good News in the Bad News?

To speak of witness and praise in the above terms seems at first glance somewhat unusual within the discourse of much contemporary evangelism. Indeed, it seems somewhat alien to vast tracks of the Christian church, especially in the West. Perhaps this is indicative of the very great challenges that confront the contemporary church: its sense of powerlessness in the modern world; its striving after new strategies for engagement and its lack of confidence in the sheer abundance of God's presence; perhaps its haunting suspicion that God is really absent (Farley 1975:1–23) or certainly displaced (Gunton 1993:11–40). The problem is one that the Christian church shares with the wider culture, which, in the words of the Jewish writer Abraham Heschel, finds it "easy to convey the resentments" but "hard to communicate praise" (Neusner 1990:190f). Heschel laments the fact that "we have nearly lost the art of conveying to our children our power to praise, our ability to cherish the things that cannot be quantified" (ibid.).

Does a praise-centered evangelism have the resources to

respond to such suspicions and anxieties? Perhaps a definite answer cannot be given, for Christian discipleship is
essentially performative rather than simply theoretical. The
viability of the way of praise, like the credibility of the
truth of Christianity, cannot be proven but requires exper-
imental grounding. This practical wisdom is well captured
in the advice of the nineteenth-century poet and theologian
Samuel Taylor Coleridge, who suggested that the only way
to prove whether Christianity was true was to "try it" (Coleridge 1893:134). The Christian community's experiment in
praise might look quite different in each situation, the reason being that the gospel makes a world of difference in
every situation but in ways that respect the local context. In
each context there will be things that thwart and counter
the emergence of true praise, and there will be much that
masquerades under the name of praise of God but in reality
is simply false or hollow (Donnelly 1992).

This points to the fact that wherever and whenever
God's people respond to the gospel a counter movement to
silence the voice and paralyze the deeds that honor God's
Christlike presence seems to appear under many forms.
This counterdynamic to the gospel can be depicted in a
variety of ways. The Johannine writings of the New Testament deploy the visual image of darkness and light, the
darkness being revealed with the coming of the gospel
light (John 3:19ff; 1 John 1:5f). Quite different but relevant for our present discussion is the auditory reference in
Luke's Gospel commonly associated with the triumphal entry of Jesus into Jerusalem leading up to his betrayal and
crucifixion. As the people welcome Jesus with shouts of
Hosanna, "Some of the Pharisees in the crowd said to Jesus,
'Teacher, rebuke your disciples!'" Jesus' reply is clear and
sharp, "'I tell you . . . if they keep quiet, the stones will cry

out'" (Luke 19:39–40). This stern rebuke seems a puzzle to many commentators although from the perspective of the present discussion Jesus' words are revealing. Even if human voices were silent, the clatter of hoofs on stones would testify to the presence of the Messiah. The countermovement to the praise of Christ could not succeed; the rest of creation would still offer sounds of praise. Our poets seem to have the exegetical edge, as evidenced in Thomas Troeger's hymn/poem "The Rocks Would Shout If We Kept Still" (1994:162) and, in a different way, the Australian poet Kevin Hart, in his poem "The Stone's Prayer" (Hart 1994:89). In particular, Troeger's poetic reflection on the triumphal entry of Jesus highlights the fact that all of creation, in its own special and appropriate way, gives voice to the God who creates and sustains. This is a wholly understandable conception if we follow Calvin's view of the Holy Spirit as "cherishing the confused mass," of "suffusing the whole of creation" (Calvin, *Institutes:* Bk. 1, par. 14) or, more recently, Wolfhart Pannenberg's conception of the Holy Spirit as "force field" sustaining creation (Pannenberg 1972). Within this broad framework, human beings have their own unique calling to bear witness to the One who creates, redeems, and fulfills all things (Rom. 11:36; cf. 1 Cor. 15:28); to be, according to the American theologian Jonathan Edwards, the "consciousness" and thus the enduring "memory of the cosmos" (Jenson 1988:36). Edwards' response to this calling was developed in terms of God's beauty, a beauty focused on Christ, a beauty that evoked praise of God in a "lively community" of open and free communication (:37, 141–44).

Yet in the above we have recognized a countermovement to such a response to God's love, a movement described in terms of darkness, and silence. If we were to pursue the theme of beauty, such a movement might be depicted in terms of distortion and ugliness. Such themes relate more, it seems, to God's absence than God's presence, to fundamentally bad news rather than good news, to entrapment rather than liberation. At this point we simply have to recognize that the face of evil and sin has many forms and expressions, that there are times when the gospel compels our silence (John 19:8–10), that in the distortions, violence, and tragedies of human life the countermovement to praise seems victorious.

There are many strategies for dealing with such occurrences in life. The ancient way of the Stoics has endured in our Western culture as a time-honored method for avoiding the testing extremes of human life. The stoic temper "endures evil, suffering and death with dignity," yet "the stoic avoids the ravages and abyss of shame at the cost of the possibility of joy" (Hardy and Ford 1994:94; cf. 139–145). To the extent that so much energy is invested in ordering and thus coping with disorder, there is little room for joy and celebration, at least the excessive kind that would overturn the much-prized and hard-won harmonies of life. Consequently, a truly penitential and celebratory praise cannot emerge, for this would involve an immersion in the fullness of life and a corresponding relinquishment of the effort to establish control in the contingencies of life that always threaten to get out of hand. In this regard, the problem for the Pharisees who wanted Jesus to silence his followers was simply that they could not share in the delight and praise of others. The spirit of stoicism exercises a powerful influence in the modern West, a fact only confirmed by the oftentimes quite anarchic and ultimately destructive ways in which people in society seek to break out of its stranglehold through various forms of wild excess. But is this true liberation for the captives?

We ought not make light of the stoic option, for it provides an important, if not the most important, response to the trials, tragedies, suffering, pain, and violence of contemporary societies. Furthermore, from this perspective the chief danger in our proposal for a praise-centered evangelism is that it could appear overly idealistic or somewhat out of touch with the "real world." We need at this point to consider exactly how such praise-centered evangelism might embrace the fullness of life as human beings actually experience it and provide the kind of orientations required for new life in the gospel. As Leander Keck has noted, "The chief obstacle to praising God is the suffering that is not self-inflicted. Whether the innocent suffer because of natural disasters (like earthquakes) or because the consequences of human folly (like wars and revolutions) do not fall only on the guilty, the burden is so heavy that praising God seems not only out of the question but also a violation of our moral sense" (1993:31). However, Keck goes on to note that "in the mysterious ecology of joy and suffering, goodness and mercy can, and often do, appear even in suffering" (:32). Although this does not lead to a requirement of praise by those "whose lives are twisted by suffering," a "monstrous" proposal for Keck, nevertheless "the Christian community dares to praise the God who did not exempt Jesus from the agony of the cross but let him share undeserved suffering with us" (ibid.). Consequently, "in the light of Jesus we also believe that in the midst of suffering, when a Ms. Job urges the sufferer to curse God and die, true praise may be silence" (:33). Thus Keck concludes that praising God "is the ultimate 'Nevertheless'! It is the supreme act of faith" (ibid.). Yet it is an act of faith that may require of the pilgrim utter silence, for silence too has its place in the ecology of Christian praise. It involves the recognition that, in a post-Holocaust world, we do not have all the answers to evil and the mystery of suffering. Perhaps, like Job and even more so Christ, in his passion and experience of godforsakenness on the cross, the Christian church can, at times, do no more than offer its praise to God in the form of an unfathomable silence.

Keck's remarks have taken us into the heartlands of the difficult area of theodicy, the justification of God in the wake of suffering and evil. His conclusions resonate with the perceptive discussion of this topic by Hardy and Ford: "So the truth about evil, suffering and death leads into the heart of who God is, and it is only through praising and knowing him that their paralyzing grip on thought as well as the rest of living can be satisfactorily released. A theodicy of praise recognizes the vindication of God by God, but this by no means allows the problem of evil to be dismissed or forgotten. Rather, it places the cross and continuing discipleship at the center of a faith which lives in a world of evil but fights with confidence in a crucified and risen Lord" (:106). This is the marrow of the gospel and a criterion for all evangelism in the name of Christ.

The above discussion suggests that the fact of evil and suffering ought not, in principle at least, overturn the centrality of praise. In fact, such realities actually provoke forms of praise that, as Keck reminds us, might include a purposeful silence. It should be a great cause for reflection that it has been out of the most difficult experiences of oppression, in which the countermovement to praise seemed unassailable, that the evangel has taken root and generated new life, hope, and liberation. The early church knew well the import of the saying "the blood of the martyrs is the seed of the church." In contexts of pain and suffering of our own times the Spirit of Pentecost has given birth to twentieth-century Pentecostalism, a movement that, in the words of F. D. Bruner, is "almost synonymous" with mission (Bruner 1970:32). In this respect it is interesting, to say the least, that "the tap-root [of Pentecostalism] was the 'invisible institution' of slave religion. That could not avoid the reality of the cross, and faced it squarely, but also took it up into the praise of the crucified Jesus" (Hardy and Ford 1984:68).

Praise-Centered Evangelism: A Real Possibility?

The note of authentic joy in God associated with the worldwide phenomenon of Pentecostalism is unmistakable. Evidently, a praise of God is possible from the most unlikely places and the most unlikely people. In one sense this should not be surprising at all, for the gospel itself is a proclamation that the God of Jesus Christ is the One who gives life to the dead, that is, to all those who have "descended to the dead." The Roman Catholic theologian Hans Urs von Balthasar interprets this christologically in relation to that strange and largely ignored article in the Apostles' Creed, "He descended to the dead" (Balthasar 1990:148–88). In von Balthasar's view this article stands as a reminder that Jesus too entered into the state of being dead—utter nothingness and solitariness — and from that state was raised by the Father and became a lifegiving Spirit (1 Cor. 15:45). Consequently, our own fall into the abyss of nothingness can be, at the same time, a fall into the arms of God whose loving reach extends beyond our imagining (Pickard 1996). The conclusion is clear: the Christian gospel is not about half-alive people or those with only a flicker of life being restored. Rather, the good news is that God creates new people and communities out of nothing — a wholly unsurprising statement given that the main character of the gospel is Jesus Christ, the crucified Lord of glory (1 Cor. 2:8). This constitutes good news, for it indicates that at the heart of the gospel is a confidence that praise of God is a real possibility even from the depths of human existence. Moreover, it is a praise that is focused on Christ and buoyed along in the same Spirit that raised Jesus from the dead.

Conclusion

The foregoing discussion suggests that the Christian tradition of the gospel does witness to the rich resources available for the recovery of right praise of God and a right honoring of persons, society, and creation. A praise-centered evangelism has, historically at least, shown itself able to embrace the full extremes of human life in this world. But, and the but is critical, the praise that emerges from such places can never be cheap praise. We recall here Dietrich Bonhoeffer's sharp words that there can be no such thing as cheap grace. The praise of God that emerges in our Western world today, if it is to be truly the praise of the God of the gospel, cannot be a cheap imitation of the crucified Lord of glory. True praise of God is usually hard won; it belongs to the dynamic identified earlier wherein "penitential praise" and "celebratory praise" operate in mutually complementary ways. This complementarity is easily lost when the dynamic aborts in favor of one or the other pole in praise. This is reflected in evangelism that proclaims, for example, a prosperity gospel and fails to take seriously wider social responsibilities. This amounts to good news for the fortunate, traditionally termed the "elect." It occurs when

a vibrant prophetic evangelism becomes ensnared in the social and political realities in such a way that it loses heart for
celebration of God in the midst. It occurs when evangelism
portrays a God whose fundamental character is lawlike, who
accordingly expects and extracts obedience from all would-
be followers. The penitent never rises into the fullness of
praise; there is little opportunity for truly *joyful* obedience.
The gospel of Jesus Christ challenges such distortions.

We are reminded at this point of Walter Brueggemann's
insight from the Psalms that "Praise is relentlessly polemi-
cal. . . . As this God is affirmed, in the same act other gods
are dismissed as irrelevant and denied any legitimacy. As
Israel acknowledges to whom it belongs, it also asserts to
whom it does not belong" (1985:66). For the early church
this involved a struggle between the one God and Father of
Jesus Christ and the many "so-called gods . . . in heaven or
on earth" (1 Cor. 8:4–6). Praise of the one God generated
polemic and controversy in a pagan culture in which many
gods were worshiped (Grant 1986).

This matter is more urgent and more complicated when
the other "gods" have become inculturated within the self-
identity of the Christian church. This, of course, was at the
basis of Barth's prophetic exegesis of Romans within the
milieu of European liberal Protestantism at the turn of the
century. It is no less relevant as we approach the third millennium within an environment in which the religions seem
to be multiplying and flourishing. The polytheism of the
ancient world has endured under new forms. The Christian churches of the West have to take stock of this fact
and its implication of the "parity" of competing cultural
and religious forms, while at the same time attending to
the "spirituality vacuum" of their own traditions (Gilkey
1991:24ff). Finding the "Way" forward in an age of re-

ligious pluralism represents one of the main challenges confronting the Christian churches of the West. Perhaps here too the way of praise has the potential for creative forward movement for the church and its evangelistic vocation. It will be a way that keeps its focus on the God of the gospel who calls communities into being that were "no communities" (1 Pet. 2:10), even in the midst of the church! It will be a way that listens and learns afresh the ways of God in the world and responds with a penitential and celebratory praise through word and deed, worship and service. In this way the church is Spirited along in the love of Christ, bearing witness to the glad tidings of God's all-sufficient and indestructible love for the world. As the church's evangelism allows itself to become caught up in the slipstream of such a gospel, captives find liberation and enter into the yearning of the whole creation for the consummation of the coming kingdom when "God may be all in all."

References Cited

Abraham, William. 1989. *The Logic of Evangelism.* London: Hodder & Stoughton.

Adams, James R. 1994. *So You Can't Stand Evangelism?* Boston: Cowley Publications.

Aldrich, Joseph. 1988. *Life-Style Evangelism.* Melbourne: Canterbury Press. First published 1981.

Arias, Mortimer, and Alan Johnson. 1992. *The Great Commission: Biblical Models for Evangelism.* Nashville: Abingdon Press.

Armstrong, Richard Stoll. 1979. *Service Evangelism.* Philadelphia: Westminster Press.

———. 1984. *The Pastor as Evangelist.* Philadelphia: Westminster Press.

———. 1986. *The Pastor Evangelist in Worship.* Philadelphia: Westminster Press.

Augustine, St. *Confessions.* 1961. Trans. with Introduction by R. S. Pine-Coffin. Harmondsworth: Penguin Books.

Babin, Pierre. 1991. *The New Era in Religious Communication.* Minneapolis: Augsburg Fortress Press.

Balthasar, Hans Urs von. 1990. *Mysterium Paschale: The Mystery of Easter.* Edinburgh: T. & T. Clark.

Barth, Karl. 1956(a). *Church Dogmatics: The Doctrine of the Word of God.* Edinburgh: T. & T. Clark.

———. 1956(b). *Church Dogmatics: The Doctrine of Reconciliation.* Edinburgh: T. & T Clark.

———. 1956(c). *Wolfgang Amadeus Mozart.* Grand Rapids: Eerdmans. Reprint edition 1992.

————. 1958. *Church Dogmatics: The Doctrine of Reconciliation.* Edinburgh: T. & T. Clark.

————. 1962. *Church Dogmatics. The Doctrine of Reconciliation.* Edinburgh: T. & T. Clark.

————. 1975. *Church Dogmatics: The Doctrine of the Word of God.* Edinburgh: T. & T. Clark.

————. 1968. *Credo.* London: Hodder & Stoughton.

Baum, Gregory, and Andrew Greeley, eds. 1974. The Church as Institution. *Concilium* 91.

Bellah, Robert N., et al. 1986. *Habits of the Heart: Individualism and Commitment in American Life.* Philadelphia: Harper & Row.

Boff, Leonardo. 1991. *New Evangelization: Good News to the Poor.* New York: Orbis Books.

Bonhoeffer, Dietrich. 1963. *Sanctorum Communio: A Dogmatic Inquiry into the Sociology of the Church.* London: Collins. From the third German edition. 1960; original 1930.

Brown, Raymond. 1979. *The Community of the Beloved Disciple.* New York: Paulist Press.

Browning, Don S., and Francis Schüssler Fiorenza, eds. 1992. *Habermas, Modernity, and Public Theology.* New York: Crossroad.

Brueggemann, Walter. 1985. Psalm 100. *Interpretation* 39:1:66.

————. 1988. *Israel's Praise: Doxology Against Idolatry and Ideology.* Philadelphia: Fortress Press.

————. 1993. *Biblical Perspectives on Evangelism: Living in a Three-Storied Universe.* Nashville: Abingdon Press.

Bruner, Frederik D. 1970. *A Theology of the Holy Spirit.* Grand Rapids: Eerdmans.

Busch, Eberhard, ed. 1976. *Karl Barth: His Life from Autobiographical Letters and Texts.* London: SCM Press.

Calvin, John. N.d. *Institutes.* McDill, Fla.: MacDonald Publishing Co.

Chapman, John. 1981. *Know and Tell the Gospel: The Why and How of Evangelism.* Sydney: Hodder & Stoughton.

Chopp, Rebecca S. 1991. *The Power to Speak: Feminism, Language, God.* New York: Crossroad.

Coalter, Milton J,. and Virgil Cruz, eds. 1995. *How Shall I Witness: Faithful Evangelism in the Reformed Tradition.* Louisville: Westminster/John Knox Press.

Coleman, Robert. 1986. *Evangelism at the Cutting Edge.* Old Tappan, N.J.: Fleming H. Revell Co.

————. 1987. *The Master Plan of Evangelism.* Old Tappan, N.J.: Spire Books. First published 1963.

Coleridge, Samuel Taylor. 1893. *Aids to Reflection and the Confessions of an Inquiring Spirit.* London: George Bell & Sons. From the fourth edition 1839; original 1825.

Costas, Orlando. 1989. *Liberating News: A Theology of Contextual Evangelism.* Grand Rapids: Eerdmans.

Crosby, Michael. 1988. *House of Disciples: Church, Economics and Justice in Matthew.* New York: Orbis Books.

Donnelly, Doris. 1992. Impediments to Praise in the Worshiping Community. *Worship* Vol. 66:1:37–53.

Drane, John. 1994. *Evangelism for a New Age: Creating Churches for the Next Century.* London: Marshall Pickering.

Drummond, Lewis. 1992. *The Word of the Cross: A Contemporary Theology of Evangelism.* Nashville: Broadman Press.

Farley, Edward. 1975. *Ecclesial Man: A Social Phenomenology of Faith and Reality.* Philadelphia: Fortress Press.

————. 1983. *Theologia: The Fragmentation and Unity of Theological Education.* Philadelphia: Fortress Press.

Fox, Robin. 1986. *Pagans and Christians.* London: Penguin Books.

Fung, Raymond. 1992. *The Isaiah Vision: An Ecumenical Strategy for Congregational Evangelism.* Geneva: WCC Publications.

Geuss, Raymond. 1981. *The Idea of a Critical Theory.* Cambridge: Cambridge University Press.

Giddens, Anthony. 1990. *The Consequences of Modernity.* Cambridge: Polity Press.

Gilkey, Langdon. 1991. *Through the Tempest: Theological Voyages in a Pluralistic Culture.* Minneapolis: Fortress Press.

Grant, Robert. 1986. *Gods and the One God.* Philadelphia: Westminster Press.

Green, Michael. 1990. *Evangelism Through the Local Church.* London: Hodder & Stoughton.

Greenway, Roger S. and Timothy M. Monsma. 1989. *Cities: Mission's New Frontier.* Grand Rapids: Baker Book House.

Gort, Jerald. 1978. Jerusalem 1928: Mission, Kingdom and Church. *International Review of Missions* 77, no. 267:273–98.

Grove Booklets on Evangelism. 1988–93. Bramcote, U.K.: Grove Books Ltd.

Gunton, Colin. 1993. *The One, the Three, and the Many: God, Creation and the Culture of Modernity.* Cambridge: Cambridge University Press.

Gunton, Colin, and Daniel Hardy, eds. 1989. *On Being the Church: Essays on the Christian Community.* Edinburgh: T. & T. Clark.

Habermas, Jürgen. 1984. *The Theory of Communicative Action.* Vol. 1. *Reason and the Rationalization of Society.* Translated from the 1981 German edition by Thomas McCarthy. Boston: Beacon Press.

Hardy, Daniel W. 1989. Created and Redeemed Sociality. In Gunton and Hardy 1989.

———. 1989. Rationality, the Sciences and Theology. In *Keeping the Faith: Essays to Mark the Centenary of Lux Mundi.* Ed. Geoffrey Wainwright. London: SPCK.

Hardy, Daniel W. and David F. Ford. 1984. *Jubilate: Theology in Praise.* London: Darton, Longman & Todd.

Haring, Bernard. 1991. *Evangelization Today.* New York: Crossroad. First published 1974, Revised edition 1990.

Hart, Kevin. 1994. *The Oxford Book of Australian Religious Verse.* Melbourne: Oxford University Press.

Hauerwas, Stanley. 1981. *A Community of Character: Toward a Constructive Christian Social Ethic.* Notre Dame: University of Notre Dame Press.

———. 1983. *The Peaceable Kingdom: A Primer in Christian Ethics.* London: SCM Press.

Heron, Alistair. 1983. *The Holy Spirit.* Philadelphia: Westminster Press.

Hunter, George G. 1992. *How to Reach Secular People.* Nashville: Abingdon Press.

Jenson, Robert W. 1988. *America's Theologian: A Recommendation of Jonathan Edwards.* New York: Oxford University Press.

Johnson, Ben Campbell. 1987. *Rethinking Evangelism: A Theological Approach.* Philadelphia: Westminster Press.

———. 1991. *Speaking of God: Evangelism as Initial Spiritual Guidance.* Louisville: Westminster/John Knox Press.

Johnson, Elizabeth. 1993. *She Who Is: The Mystery of God in Feminist Theological Discourse.* New York: Crossroad.

Jossua, Jean-Pierre. 1985. *The Condition of the Witness.* London: SCM Press. From the French edition 1984.

Keck, Leander E. 1993. *The Church Confident.* Nashville: Abingdon Press.

Kelly, Tony. 1989. *The Trinity of Love: A Theology of the Christian God.* Wilmington, Del.: Michael Glazier.

Kennedy, D. James. 1972. *Evangelism Explosion.* London: Coverdale House. Original 1970.

Kerr, Hugh T. 1991. *The Simple Gospel: Reflections on Christian Faith.* Louisville: Westminster/John Knox Press.

Kolb, Robert. 1984. *Speaking the Gospel Today: A Theology of Evangelism.* St. Louis: Concordia Publishing House.

Lakeland, Paul. 1990. *Theology and Critical Theory: The Discourse of the Church.* Nashville: Abingdon Press.

Larsen, David. 1992. *The Evangelism Mandate: Recovering the Centrality of Gospel Preaching.* Wheaton, Ill.: Crossway Books.

Lindbeck, George A. 1984. *The Nature of Doctrine: Religion and Theology in a Postliberal Age.* London: SPCK.

Lovell, Arnold. 1990. *Evangelism in the Reformed Tradition.* Decatur, Ga.: CTS.

Marshall, Michael. 1990. *The Gospel Connection.* Wilton, Conn.: Morehouse Publishing.

McFadyen, Alistair. 1990. *The Call to Personhood: A Christian Theory of the Individual in Social Relationships.* Cambridge: Cambridge University Press.

McGavran, Donald A. 1988. *Effective Evangelism: A Theological Mandate.* Phillipsburg, N.J.: Presbyterian and Reformed Publishing Company.

Moltmann, Jürgen. 1978. *The Open Church.* London: SCM Press.

———. 1981. *The Trinity and the Kingdom of God.* London: SCM Press.

Mudge, Lewis. 1992. *The Sense of a People: Toward a Church for the Human Future.* Philadelphia: Trinity Press International.

Neave, Rosemary. 1992. *Gossiping the Gospel: Women Reflect on Evangelism.* Auckland, N.Z.: The Women's Resource Centre.

Neusner, Jacob. 1990. *To Grow in Wisdom: An Anthology of Abraham Joshua Heschel.* New York: Madison Books.

Newbigin, Lesslie. 1989. *The Gospel in a Pluralist Society.* London: SPCK.

Niedenthal, Morris. 1980. The Irony and Grammar of the Gospel. In *Preaching the Story.* Ed. Edmund Steimle, Morris Niedenthal, and Charles Rice. Philadelphia: Fortress Press.

Pannenberg, Wolfhart. 1972. The Doctrine of the Spirit and the Task of a Theology of Nature. *Theology* 75:8–21.

———. 1991. *Systematic Theology.* Vol. 1. Grand Rapids: Eerdmans.

Pelikan, Jaroslav. 1988. *The Christian Tradition: Christian Doctrine and Modern Culture* (since *1700).* Chicago and London: University of Chicago Press.

Peters, Ted. 1993. *God as Trinity: Relationality and Temporality in Divine Life.* Louisville: Westminster/John Knox Press.

Pickard, Stephen. 1993. Evangelism and the Character of Christian Theology. *Missionalia* 21:2 (Aug.):159–75.

———. 1996. He Descended to the Dead: Can this Article of Faith be Resurrected? *Ministry: Journal for Continuing Education* 6 (Autumn):4–6.

Pomerville, Paul A. 1985. *The Third Force in Missions: A Pentecostal Contribution to Contemporary Mission Theology.* Peabody, Mass.: Hendrickson.

Pope-Levison, Priscilla. 1991. *Evangelization from a Liberation Perspective.* New York: Peter Lang.

Posterski, Donald C. 1989. *Reinventing Evangelism: Strategies for Preserving Christ in Today's World.* Downers Grove, Ill.: Inter-Varsity Press.

Rahner, Karl. 1970. *The Trinity.* London: Burns & Oates.

———. 1978. *Foundations of Christian Faith: An Introduction to the Idea of Christianity.* London: Darton, Longman & Todd.

Rainer, Thomas S., ed. 1989. *Evangelism in the Twenty-First Century.* Wheaton, Ill.: Harold Shaw Publishers.

Ricoeur, Paul. 1975. Paul Ricoeur on Biblical Hermeneutics. *Semeia* 4. NB Volume 4 of Semeia was written by Ricoeur as above.

Roberts, Richard. 1996. A Postmodern Church? Some Preliminary Reflections on Ecclesiology and Social Theory. In *Essentials of Christian Community*. Ed. David F. Ford and Dennis L. Stamps. Edinburgh: T. & T. Clark.

Rudnick, Milton. 1984. *Speaking the Gospel Through the Ages: A History of Evangelism*. St. Louis: Concordia Publishing House.

Ruffcorn, Kevin. 1994. *Rural Evangelism: Catching the Vision*. Minneapolis: Augsburg Fortress Press.

Schaff, Philip. 1990. *The Creeds of Christendom*. Vol. 3. Grand Rapids: Baker Book House.

Schillebeeckx, Edward. 1988. *The Church with a Human Face*. New York: Crossroad.

Scherer, James A., and Stephen B. Bevans. 1992. *New Directions in Mission and Evangelization. Vol. 1. Basic Statements 1974–1991*. New York: Orbis Books.

Schleiermacher, Friedrich. 1960. *The Christian Faith*. Edinburgh: T. & T. Clark. From the 1928 English translation the of second German edition 1830.

Shenk, Wilbert. 1995. *Write the Vision: The Church Renewed*. Valley Forge, Pa.: Trinity Press International.

Stendahl, Krister. 1973. The Apostle Paul and the Introspective Conscience of the West. *Harvard Theological Review* 56:199–215.

Sternberg, Robert J., ed. 1990. *Wisdom: Its Nature, Origins, and Development*. Cambridge: Cambridge University Press.

Sykes, Stephen W. 1984. *The Identity of Christianity*. London: SPCK.

———. 1991. An Anglican Theology of Evangelism. *Theology* 94 (Nov./Dec. 1991):405–14.

Taylor, Mark C. 1984. *Erring: A Postmodern A/theology*. London and Chicago: University of Chicago Press.

Tillich, Paul. 1968. *Systematic Theology*. Vol. 3. Digswell Place, Herts., U.K.: James Nisbet & Co. Ltd.

Trible, Phyllis. 1978. *God and the Rhetoric of Sexuality*. Philadelphia: Fortress Press.

Troeger, Thomas. 1994. *Borrowed Light: Hymn Texts, Prayers and Poems.* New York: Oxford University Press.

UCA. 1994. *Ordination and Ministry in the Uniting Church.* Sydney: Uniting Church National Assembly.

Wainwright, Geoffrey. 1980. *Doxology: The Praise of God in Worship, Doctrine and Life.* London: Epworth Press.

Wilden, Anthony. 1980. *System and Structure: Essays in Communication and Exchange.* 2nd ed. London: Tavistok Publications.

Wimber, John. 1985. *Power Evangelism: Signs and Wonders Today.* London: Hodder & Stoughton.